YOU ARE BEAUTIFUL

A Model Makeover *from* Insecure *to* Confident in Christ

ASHLEY REITZ

with Lorilee Craker

Faith Words

New York   Nashville

FaithWords
Hachette Book Group
1290 Avenue of the Americas, New York, NY 10104
faithwords.com
twitter.com/faithwords

Originally published in hardcover and ebook in December 2017
First trade paperback edition: December 2018

FaithWords is a division of Hachette Book Group, Inc. The FaithWords name and logo are trademarks of Hachette Book Group, Inc.

The publisher is not responsible for websites (or their content) that are not owned by the publisher.

The Hachette Speakers Bureau provides a wide range of authors for speaking events. To find out more, go to www.hachettespeakersbureau.com or call (866) 376-6591.

Library of Congress Cataloging-in-Publication Data

Names: Reitz, Ashley, author. | Craker, Lorilee, author.
Title: You are beautiful : a model makeover from insecure to confident in Christ / Ashley Reitz with Lorilee Craker.
Description: First edition. | New York : Faith Words, [2017] | Includes bibliographical references.
Identifiers: LCCN 2017029728| ISBN 9781478975687 (hardcover) | ISBN 9781478923596 (audio download) | ISBN 9781478975694 (ebook)
Subjects: LCSH: Christian women--Religious life. | Beauty, Personal—Religious aspects--Christianity.
Classification: LCC BV4527 .R444 2017 | DDC 248.8/43--dc23
LC record available at https://lccn.loc.gov/2017029728

ISBNs: 978-1-4789-7570-0 (trade paperback), 978-1-4789-7569-4 (ebook)

Printed in the United States of America

LSC-C

10 9 8 7 6 5 4 3 2 1

*To the most beautiful woman I have
ever encountered: my mom.
Thank you for showing me what true
beauty is in a world that so easily forgets.
And to my niece, Makenna, whose
little life changed mine.
You gave me the drive to write the
messages in this book,
and my hope is that you will grow up
knowing what true beauty is.*

CONTENTS

INTRODUCTION

You are beautiful—do you believe it?

I spent most of my twenty-eight years believing the opposite—that I was too chubby, boring, unseen and overlooked, not special, not *enough*. But then I underwent an emotional and spiritual transformation in my life, a "model makeover" from insecure to confident in Christ. In these pages, my heart's desire is to help *you* discover that you, too, are loved and oh so beautiful.

I want to walk with you, as a friend and big sis, to show you the path to true wholeness, peace, and body acceptance. Are you ready?

This book is for you if you sometimes feel like you are not thin/pretty/good enough. You'll hear my story in its rawest, most vulnerable form, in the hope that you won't feel so alone anymore. Because, despite being a good girl and even a pastor's daughter, I took some destructive detours in unhealthy dieting and beauty and body obsession before discovering that I was already special and good enough—because Jesus had made me so.

Here are my stories of growing up feeling overweight and unnoticed, woven with behind-the-scenes snapshots of the good, the bad, and the ugly of the modeling industry. Here are lessons for you on how to find true confidence as you discover your identity in Christ, not the empty substitutes of this world.

For me, the pursuit of "empty substitutes" began early in life. When I was just twelve years old, I begged my mom to let me and my sisters try out to be runway models at an upcoming mall spring fashion show. The moment I found out not only that I had been overlooked but that both my sisters had been chosen was defining for me—I realized I would have to try much harder to be thin, pretty, lovable…and wanted.

I struggled on and off for years, into young adulthood, with an unrealistic body image and disordered eating that left me unhealthy and miserable. Like so many of you, I often wondered why my personal faith and God's love failed to fill the gaping chasm in my soul. *Why do some of my ugliest, most anxious, and most vulnerable moments take place in church?* Have you ever questioned the same thing?

Even after I grew up and plunged into my beloved beauty school and a successful international modeling career, it took personal tragedy, including a terrifying assault, to provide me with the needed clarity and strength to confront my profound insecurities. I realized I had to surrender daily, actively seeking my acceptance and finding my worth in Jesus alone.

As together we explore topics of confidence, beauty, positive body image, and the maddening—and futile—pursuit of perfection, I pray this book speaks truth and healing into your life! Together, we will go to some dark places, because sometimes you have to go back to go forward. Places where we are feeling…unseen.

UNSEEN

Have you ever felt like if you disappeared, no one would even notice you were gone? I can identify. I grew up with a lot of love and support in my family, but as a middle child between perfect, tiny sisters and a rowdy brother who drew attention like a heat-seeking missile, I often felt unseen. It didn't help that I was the plump, "big boned" one or that I felt I had to share my parents not only with my three siblings but with my dad's church members.

It all added up to a sense of being unnoticed, or at least unseen for my gifts and qualities. I can't tell you where this feeling came from, but I felt it. I think we all do, am I right? We long to be singled out as special. We crave the interest of those we love and admire, their awareness and consideration of us is so vital. Yet it's so easy to feel lost in the middle of a busy family, school, church, or workplace.

OVERLOOKED

We can't talk about feeling unseen without discussing a related but distinct emotion: rejection, feeling unchosen, uninvited, and unwanted. It's one thing to *feel* invisible sometimes and another to have that impression *verified* by the rejections of this world. Because when we get the cold shoulder instead of a warm hug, it hurts!

Been there, done that, have the T-shirt! For years and years, I bought into the lie that somehow I *wasn't* enough, that there was something about me that was essentially overlookable. Can you relate?

A little preview of chapter 2: Jesus understands what it is to be overlooked. No matter how coldly we've been rejected, or how overwhelmingly we've been snubbed, we can find hope and strength in the God who gets it—and gets us.

In these pages, we will delve into what it means to live in a world which has us on a treadmill, killing ourselves to be pretty.

PRETTY

There's nothing wrong with wanting to be pretty. In fact, we were created with an innate desire to be desirable, wanted. And if you're one of those girls who loves nothing more than makeover night, reveling in the newest shades of blush and nail polish, ain't nothing wrong with that either! You may encounter resistance from others, especially those inside the church, who say your interest in beauty is vain and not befitting a "good Christian girl." I had that kind of pushback too (see chapter 3). The key is to be a pretty-*does* girl, treating others as precious image bearers of God, and putting your Father's kingdom far above all else.

We also want to be skinny.

SKINNY

Wow—do we ever want to be skinny! This chapter hits close to the bone, going deep into my weight issues and all weight issues. The truth I came to the hard way was that "healthy" is a feeling, not a look. But first I had to make peace with the body God gave me.

BEAUTIFUL

I learned that our Father pays close attention to what's inside. He already sees us as beautiful.

Yes, beautiful.

There's a reason this plummy pink book you are holding in your hands is not called "You Are Pretty." Yes, we talk about the pursuit of prettiness in chapter 3, and about being a "pretty-does" kind of girl, but pretty pales in comparison to beautiful.

So many things can be beautiful without having a thing to do with long eyelashes or one's BMI. *You* are beautiful. The truth is, the most beautiful people in the world are those who see the beauty in others, even when it's hidden. Our Father sees the "hidden person of the heart," as Peter puts it in 1 Peter 3:4 (ESV). The hidden person of your heart is precious to God, so let's challenge our culture's narrow definition of beauty to find the truth that will change our lives. We will never be the same once we find out we are beautiful.

Yes, you are beautiful and were created by God to have an exclusive, exceptional significance. Your life's purpose is elite.

ELITE

Really? Yeah, I didn't buy it at first either. Not for way too long. For years, I pinned my sense of worth on whether or not I would cut my weight, that boy would finally crush on me, or that dream would come true at long last. But I learned something (else) the hard way. If you can't find meaning, value, and approval from within—the person made and loved by God—it's going to be even harder to find it when placed into the hands of someone else.

For so long I searched for my life's purpose and affirmation in other people's eyes. Can you identify? We've all been there. Reaching into Queen Esther's magnificent story, we'll discover where true purpose and affirmation comes from. The goals of this world may feel good—even amazing—for a time, but they deliver a short-lived satisfaction. When you realize you were pursued by a King for *your* singular purpose, your elite reason for being, you take another step into your story of freedom.

Before we stride into our freedom, however, we have to uncover the inner urge so many of us have.

STRIVE

In chapter 7 we'll commiserate together, because the quest for perfection in our world is crazy-making—and endless. Every day there is something new to chase after, some new look, weight, answer, thing, or person. And we wonder all the while, *Why am I so imperfect?*

We've all pretended, performed, and tried to prove ourselves in unhealthy ways. I have pretended I had it all together when I didn't. I'm betting you have too. Isn't the pressure something else? But that's not how our Father built us to live, carrying the heavy burden of trying to be enough. He wants you to leave your striving at the curb. He wants you to travel lightly!

Lightly? Sounds perfect, but how can you travel lightly when circumstances in your life are weighing you down? Things *will* fall apart, if you're human. We all suffer. In chapter 8, I open up about my terrible, no good, awful year.

SLIDE

You've also suffered, I'm sure. Maybe someone you love died, leaving you in pieces. Or maybe it was a different kind of loss, the loss of a relationship or job. A run of bad luck, when it seemed that you couldn't get a win to save your life. Times like these can bring you down and cause you to question everything you believe in.

During my slide, I clung to the cliff and tried to hang on, to no avail. (I was ignoring the fact that cliffs crumble, but the Rock of our salvation does not!)

But then there was a curve in the right direction.

CURVE

Sadly, after my terribly hard year, I forgot that I was held. I forgot the truth. Actually, I pushed it out of my mind as hard as I could. So at first, my path curved away from Him. I was depressed, anxious, and fighting to hold on to what I believed in.

Was there ever a season in your life where you felt

as though you were wrestling with God? Take it from me—the struggle is useless, and you are going to be utterly sapped by the effort. I learned that when life throws us curves, we need to bend *toward* Him.

He is making all things new, and He always has a plot twist in mind for His girls. The plot twist He had for me blew my mind. I never thought in a million years I would be the kind of girl to be on a reality dating show, but that's exactly where the curved road ended up!

REALITY

In chapter 10, we'll take a peek behind the scenes of TV dating—it probably won't be what you expect. My journey on *Coupled* and my relationship with the man I met there was far deeper and more complex than I imagined.

God was with me every step of the way. He used an unreal situation in my life to show me what was real, and He longs to show *you* your real and valid identity in Him. When we start to believe in our worth and value, everything changes, including our relationships with men, or our lack of relationships with men. Coupled or uncoupled, God has to be the authentic heartbeat of our lives.

CONFIDENT

Finally, we'll work out what it means to be biblically confident, not sure of ourselves, but sure of Him; not self-reliant but utterly dependent on our Father.

As I chronicle my makeover from insecure to confident in Christ, my dearest hope is that you are with me, soaking in the truth of your God-infused identity, and transforming along the way.

You are beautiful! You might not believe it yet—but you will.

YOU

ARE

BEAUTIFUL

1
UNSEEN

*H*ave you ever felt like if you vanished into thin air, no one would even notice you were gone? I can relate. I grew up with a lot of love and support and wouldn't trade my tribe for anything. Still, as a middle child between perfect, petite sisters and a rambunctious brother, I often felt unseen, unnoticed. It didn't help that I was the chubby one.

Anyone out there a middle child? I see you! I notice you! As the second of four children I completely understand the "middle child syndrome." My older sister, Andrea, was practically perfect in all she did. She always earned above a 4.0 in school, conquered anything she put her mind to (hello, college scholarship queen), and always followed the house rules, church rules, school rules…you get the picture.

My younger brother, Mike, should have been my lifelong companion in the middle of our family, but, well, he was the only boy in the house and quite honestly took more energy for my parents to raise than all three girls combined. Mike required nonstop surveillance. The neighbors across the street used to look over and witness Mike jumping from couch to couch. *Bless Gene and Robin for being able to raise that kid,* they would think to themselves.

And then of course there was baby Lauren. "Tiny Peanut" who was fawned over 24/7 by everyone for just how perfect her little angel self was.

Me? Thank you for wondering. Usually you could find me in a quiet corner of the house, daydreaming, painting furniture with nail polish, using the family video camera to make a music video, or cutting the hair of my dolls or baby sister. I knew I was loved and cared for, but I still craved attention. I wanted to be seen as someone special, yet I knew at an early age it was always going to be a challenge to stand out, to be noticed. Like every middle child ever, I had to compete for family attention against the milestones set by my sister, the rowdiness of my brother, and the adorable sweetness of my baby sister. Without being able to articulate it then, I longed for the family spotlight.

Being a pastor's kid (aka PK) did not help either. You might think being the child of a pastor would bring with it lots of attention, but it wasn't always the good kind of attention. The phone rang at all hours, with my dad's congregants on the other end needing something from him, from us (because when he had to dash off from dinner or from helping one of us with our homework, it took something from us). On one hand, I was blessed to learn so much about Christ and His love, but I also shared my parents with not only three siblings at home but over a hundred other "siblings" in the family of God! On many occasions, I felt their needs trumped mine, and besides that, I felt uncomfortable with the high expectations of how I should dress, behave, talk, and later, post on social media.

When I became a teenager, I would experience even more pressure as I usually fell short of the stock image of the perfect pastor's daughter. I was frustrated at the hypocrisy and didn't feel that many of the church members really cared for me beyond a surface level, yet I watched my parents commit their lives to helping them. Whether my perceptions were right or wrong, for me, church wasn't where I went to find belonging. It felt like a lonely place.

It all added up to a general impression of being unseen, or at least unseen for my gifts and qualities. I can't tell you where this feeling came from, but I felt it. I think we all do. We long to be seen and noticed. We pine for that feeling of being special, not lost in the middle of a busy family, school, church, or workplace. We want to be singled out in the best possible way, and made to feel as if we have deep value, just for being us. I knew I could never be petite and adorable like my sisters, or pose the constant threat of burning down the house like my brother, so the question smoldered in my heart and mind: How could I possibly become visible and noticeable to those around me?

Mary Kay Ash, the famous makeup and skincare guru, liked to say, "Everyone has an invisible sign hanging around their neck saying, 'Make me feel important.'" She lived by this motto and creed, and wanted all her sales people to take note and live by it too. I love this saying, because it's so insightful into human nature, and it reminds me that I have the power to boost someone's spirits and make them feel special.

I also know it's so easy to fall into the trap of using cheap substitutes to make us feel important. When we get a hit of acceptance from someone who is popular, it feels so good and that void is filled for a little while. When a cute guy gives us some attention, we get caught up *so quickly* with the amazing feeling of being wanted. And then there's social media. There's a high that comes with watching the number of likes go up on a photo you posted.

There are full-on companies now completely centered on teaching people how to grow our social media followings. You can actually hire people to "make you look good" to ensure you get the most likes, retweets, shares, etc.

One of the issues I have with social media is the immediate gratification it can provide. "That post got tons of likes, so I am going to keep posting more of the same so I can feel this good again next time I post." Or the opposite can be just as true. When we post something meaningful to us—a photo, a quote, a meme— and barely anyone even seems to register or care, we feel a sense of discontentment and emptiness. *Why aren't the people around me noticing my post? Why don't they see me?* And our feelings of invisibility intensify until we can figure out a way to be "worthy" of notice again. It can all be so fast and so faux!

Let me tell you, cheap substitutes can be like cheap beauty products and half-baked or rushed treatments. They seem like they might fit the bill in the moment, but whoa, they can backfire in a big way! My brother's wedding, for example, was one of those occasions where I went for the fast and the faux, and it cost me. You see, I was throwing a bit of a pity party for myself. I mean, who wants to be the older sister attending baby bro's wedding solo? Am I right? In my pitiful fog, I thought there were only two options to help me feel a little less sorry for myself: (1) Show up a little more blonde, or (2) show up a little more tan.

You know, so people wouldn't look at me and say, *Ohhh, Ashley isn't looking so good. That's why she's single with no date to her little brother's wedding.*

Instead I wanted them to think, *Ohhh…Ashley is looking great and she must simply be so inundated with date requests that she couldn't have possibly chosen just one as a wedding date.* Vain fantasy, but come on…you know you'd do the same!

First there was the hair catastrophe. "A little more blonde" turned into bleachy bomb. Then I convinced myself that my horrible hair would look better with a spray tan. I mean, everything looks better with a spray tan! I had never had any problems with a spray tan before…But when I went to a new spray tan technician, I walked in as Ashley and out as Pumpkin Spice Girl. Truly! Had a casting director for *Willy Wonka* spotted me I would have been cast in the movie—as a tall Oompa Loompa. I washed, scrubbed, blended, and did everything short of taking the Brillo pad at the kitchen sink to my face until I realized I had two choices: Skip my brother's wedding, or go as a pumpkin. I went as a pumpkin. Literally, people have been heard to ask, when looking at those wedding pics, "Who's the human gourd?"

Unfortunately, I am known for making rash beauty decisions. I remember the day before my senior pictures, I turned my hair into a skunk. (There was this huge trend going on where it was really cool to have the bottom half of your head a dark color and super light on top. I think it was brought on by Christina Aguilera.) We ended up canceling those pictures and spending many hours and lots of cash just to get my head of hair back to normal. My poor mother was not pleased!

Just like a fake bake or a bottle of drugstore hair dye, trying to feel noticeable via cheap substitutes seems like a good idea at the time but never is. Most of the bargain beauty products and treatments wash off, but truly they can't change anything on the inside. The quick fixes we turn to time and time again—our "make me feel important" go-tos—do nothing to make us feel secure or imbue us with a true sense of worth. They do nothing to answer the deep questions of our souls: Am I good enough? Am I special? Does anyone see me?

Sometimes, the things we do to get validation and acceptance are good—they aren't fake or cheap. I found out in high school that through sports I was able to get noticed in a positive way. Basketball and volleyball were two sports I could play really well. My dad was a coach and I can't tell you how much joy it gave me when he praised me for how I had done in a game. Any little bit of recognition felt like that hole inside me was one step closer to getting filled. Now, there's nothing wrong with playing sports and feeling good about it. In fact, sports are super healthy and positive! The problem comes in when we find our total worth in those things, because other teams will always show up and beat the pants off you, no matter how good you are. There will always be someone who is faster, stronger, more agile, taller—you get it.

Maybe sports isn't your thing. Maybe you light up like a Broadway show when you act or sing or dance or write or take photographs. God gives His girls good gifts, and loves it when we light up like that. But while an accolade or pat on the back for a job well done can make us feel understood and appreciated for a little while, eventually the feeling will "wash off" like my spray tan finally did.

Have you ever felt like your attempts to get people to notice you end up giving you deeper feelings of insecurity than before? Trying to keep up with the wealthier girls at my private school in terms of clothes and other possessions left me feeling worse than ever about my own humble clothing budget. The more I tried, the more I spun on a hamster wheel, revolving in circles and never getting anywhere. It's like those prize machines you see at arcades, where you put in quarter after quarter trying to get something, but you never really win, do you? You try for that one pink teddy bear and realize after wasting twelve quarters you should probably try for something different. So you move on to the blue bunny and you think surely you'll be able to reach that one. And the process goes on until you've spent all your money, and you finally realize that stupid claw will never actually allow you to win! That was me. Wasting all my quarters just trying the next new beauty product, trend, or achievement that would hopefully allow me to win my classmates' attention.

I honestly thought modeling would thrust me into the spotlight and thus make me feel like a million bucks. I mean, how better to be out there in plain sight than to have people take your photograph and splash it in magazines and catalogues? I would be visible to hundreds of thousands of folks around the country and even the world—no more feeling insignificant or unworthy for me! Or at least that's what I thought at the start.

When I found out I'd be working with Russell James, the well-known Victoria's Secret/Kendall Jenner photographer, I could hardly believe my ears. I was going to be on a shoot for Avon—you know, the catalogs that our moms always used to get on a weekly basis with yummy nail polish and lip colors to admire? Before I flew out for this job, my agent looked at me and said, "This is a big deal! You were chosen out of hundreds of other models. Make us proud."

Seeing James at the studios of Chelsea Piers in New York City was a moment I'll never forget. He had a very calm demeanor, and at the same time I could sense how well he was respected as a celebrity photographer because of how he clearly called the shots. Everyone around him instantly obeyed his every quiet utterance. He was very pleasant to work with, and I was thankful. Believe me, you can't say that about every photographer. Some make your insecurities flare up instead of calm down!

Another model, a straight-size Latina from Miami, and I were escorted through security and spent time in hair and makeup in our fancy robes. It was a beautiful set and a surreal opportunity, but I felt very uncomfortable. First of all, it was just me, a normal-size girl with some extra around her midsection, and Estrella, whose size 0–2 body was seen as perfect in the eyes of the fashion and beauty industry.

Oh, get over it, you might be thinking. *You're a model!* I get you, but hear me out. I represent *curve* bodies, which means I am a model with cellulite, stretch marks, rolls, and the insecurities that go with those things. And in this setting, with that photographer and that girl, I felt the opposite of invisible. I felt like all thirty people on that shoot could see my body's flaws through a magnifying glass.

Everything in me screamed, "I'm so embarrassed right now. I want to run. I want to hide!" I dared not show it, though. I kept remembering the words from my agent: "Make us proud."

Also, it wasn't like we were wearing parkas. Pretty much a sports bra. Nothing seductive because I won't do that type of work. Yet the clothes I was modeling did not offer as much coverage as I would have liked, adding to my discomfort. In my mind, every one of my fat cells was jumping up and down yelling, "Hey, check me out! Take my picture! Take a group picture! We are having a convention on Ashley's left thigh!" The irony was that one of the driving forces behind my becoming a model in the first place was so I could be seen; no more white crayon on white paper! And here I was, at a peak moment in my career, and everything in me wanted to hide.

During a lunch break, the other model, Estrella, came and sat next to me. We had a great time chatting and getting to know each other. I started to relax a bit and loosen up. This girl was just like me! I checked myself and thought, *Stop thinking you are somehow less than Estrella because she's "perfect" and stop thinking you are more flawed by the minute.* Instead of allowing myself to further spiral down into an insecure puddle, I decided to challenge my thoughts:

- I don't care about how this situation makes me *feel*.
- I am *choosing* to throw all those self-defeating thoughts down the drain.
- I am *here* because God wants me to be here and I will do my job confidently, in His strength!

As I sat on my flight later that day I couldn't stop thinking about the day's roller coaster of emotions. I thought about how I had tamed my insecurities, for just a moment. Could I do this every time I had a vulnerable, exposed moment like that until I truly owned my feelings and didn't let my feelings own me?

Have you ever had the start to a good day, when suddenly someone's verbal comment or post on Instagram suddenly makes you feel bad about yourself? Something or someone triggers the feeling of being unseen. You feel invisible in your family, at school, where you work, even in your relationships. It's an awful feeling, like no one seems to know—or care—that you're there.

I still get hijacked by those feelings of unworthiness; we all do. Those little lies hiss in our ears and feed our negative thoughts about ourselves.

I will never capture the attention of _____ (fill in the blank—the popular group, a boy, your parents) because of...

- my new epic zit.
- my weight.
- my boring personality.

And on and on it goes. That's why we have to challenge our thoughts, as I did when I felt so insignificant next to Estrella on that Russell James photo shoot! We have to grab that steering wheel from the lies and steer ourselves back onto the path of worth and value. God always holds us close in plain sight—but we forget that constantly, don't we? I know I do. When the lies and the triggers come and our worth feels shaky, it's time to remind ourselves of our inherent beauty, worth, and value.

We are noticeable! We are loved. *You* are worth noticing and loved tenderly.

But how do we even start to challenge these rampant thoughts? Job one is to check our self-talk. That's right—all the talking we do with ourselves (mind you, this is internal talking, not the way we all talk to ourselves in the car or the kitchen or walking down the street). The truth is, we talk to ourselves more than we talk to anyone else. And the most important words we will ever say to another human being are the words we use for ourselves.

According to David Stoop, author of *Self-Talk: Key to Personal Growth*,[1] we talk out loud at the rate of 150–200 words per minute. Some of us talk more (hands raised?), and some us talk a little less. But get this: Our inner self-talk is 1,300 words per minute!

When we yammer on and on to ourselves about how chubby and ugly we are, how uninteresting, invisible, hidden, unseen, worthless, there is so much harmful content pouring into our sensitive spirits. We begin to believe the lies and then behave accordingly. When those defeating, invisible-making thoughts invade our minds, we have to stop and do the work, just even for a few seconds. It doesn't mean sitting in time-out for five minutes and meditating. But it does mean mentally shutting down those poisonous thoughts before they spread.

Good, Bible-based God talk is the healing cure for a bruised heart. Think of good self-talk as a way of flushing your spirit of the world's daily damaging input. By addressing ourselves and speaking words that are clean, true, positive, and pure, it rinses our hearts and minds of junk fuel and fills us with power and love.

Taking five minutes in the morning and then again at night to purposely wash out the negative influences helps clean out our internal systems. When circumstances and people are making you feel like shrinking into a little ball, remind yourself right then and there of your value. In those few seconds after that icky feeling pops up, say something like this, out loud or inaudibly: "I feel unseen and uncared for, but it's just not true, and this is why…" (I do this often. I say it out loud when I'm in a place to do so. I just stop and say a little prayer when I'm feeling bummed about whatever it may be.)

"Lord, I feel weak right now and I'm discouraged about such and such. But I know this is not true and You created me with more value than I can comprehend. I thank You for that and I want to live in that. Thank You, Jesus, Amen."

God works in those seemingly small moments. All those little flashes of surrendering our thoughts? They fortify and solidify our identity in Him. Truth by truth, we are built up in the true value Jesus confers upon us. The more we take in that truth, the more we will rest in God's arms as beloved, joyful, and confident daughters.

Back to cheap substitutes—we may think in those moments when we feel unseen that getting a few likes on our Instagram photo or a scrap of attention from a cute guy will make us feel better, and it does, for a little, tiny while. It's like using cornstarch as a dry shampoo—it fluffs up your bangs for a few hours and then pretty soon they start drooping and out comes the baseball hat! Purposefully absorbing and assimilating God's truth about you is like lathering up with the world's most lavish, expensive shampoo, the kind that smells like watermelon, lychee, and flower extracts, and protects your hair against harmful UV radiation. It cleanses and renews, strengthens and restores your hair to its peak of beauty. When we "lather up" with God's truth, we are cleansed, renewed, strengthened, and restored.

The fact that God sees us changes everything. It means that when we feel ignored and unnoticed by a busy, broken world, we can go to Him. He is always present, reassuring us, keeping us, covering our pain in the shadow of His wings. That day on Chelsea Piers was a turning point for me. I realized that in my loneliest moments I needed to swap out cheap, shallow substitutes for the priceless, mysterious truth that fills me up and deeply satisfies.

It's like the woman with the blood disorder, in Luke 8, who trudged through life on the margins, invisible to those around her, until she encountered Jesus. Despairing, she pushed her way through the masses flooding around Jesus, believing she'd be healed if she could just touch the hem of His robe. When she did, she got her miracle.

Jesus—who's mobbed by people—says, "Someone touched me." Then comes this wonderful postscript to the story: "Then the woman, seeing that she could not go unnoticed...fell at his feet" (Luke 8:47). This frantic woman realized that day what so many have realized since. Nobody goes unnoticed by Jesus! She was filled up that day with the truth of her value in the One whose robe she touched.

We, too, get our miracle when we begin to realize just how *seen* we really are. Psalm 139 is one of my favorite chapters of the Bible. It is a treasure trove of profound, life-giving, insecurity-busting truth.

The psalmist tells us we are seen and understood:

- Before we were even born—"My frame was not hidden from you when I was made in the secret place, when I was woven together in the depths of the earth. Your eyes saw my unformed body" (v. 15–16).
- In this very moment in time—"You have searched me, LORD, and you know me. You know when I sit and when I rise; you perceive my thoughts from afar. You discern my going out and my lying down; you are familiar with all my ways" (v. 1–3).
- No matter how hard things seem or how far we wander—"If I go up to the heavens, you are there; if I make my bed in the depths, you are there. If I rise on the wings of the dawn, if I settle on the far side of the sea, even there your hand will guide me" (v. 8–10).

It's so comforting to know that we have a God who will always choose to see us and meet us where we are regardless of our mess-ups, past and present. God is ever watchful for His girls, attentive, and full of care. He whispers, "My daughter, My character is love. My name makes you lovable. Because I am worthy, I make you worthy. You are never invisible to Me."

Beauty Box

1. When was the last time you felt unseen?

2. What are your top three cheap substitutes for beauty products?

3. What are your top three quick fixes when you want to feel more noticeable?

4. Next time you feel unnoticed and unimportant, you are going to check and challenge your thoughts: *Hey girl! Don't you buy into this garbage that nobody sees you and nobody cares. Stop right there!* (In simple terms, keep the poison from spreading. Contain the oil spill!) Then you will "rinse off" and remind yourself of your worth and value in Jesus.

5. Going one step further, write down the following reminder that you are held in plain sight in God's eyes. "My daughter, My character is love. My name makes you lovable. Because I am worthy, I make you worthy. You are never invisible to Me." Twice a day, morning and night, read this and thank God for seeing you.

6. The woman who touched Jesus's robe in Luke 8 was used to no one noticing her. Let yourself be the one who thinks, *Who is there around me like that?* Start looking for those very people and make them feel that they too are worthy to be noticed and loved.

2
OVERLOOKED

I bet you, like me, can remember in excruciating detail certain episodes of your life when your heart got banged up pretty good. For whatever reason, it's those times when we felt kicked to the curb of life, completely snubbed, that can linger in our hearts for a long time after they have happened.

We've all gone through times when someone special or a person we held in high esteem obviously preferred somebody else to us.

We've all been there:

- Passed over by a teacher, a boss, a play director
- Shunned by peers, maybe even a former friend and her band of she-bullies
- Rejected by someone whose opinion mattered to you, someone with the power to break your heart

When life gives us the cold shoulder (and it will, on a regular basis), we feel so low, undeserving somehow. That's when we need to lean on the mighty shoulders of the One who always says, "I choose *you*, dear girl. My shoulder is always here for you to cry on. I will always hold you tight."

I wish someone had told me that, years ago when my heart got banged up, when I sat there on the curb of life feeling dissed and ditched. I mean, as a pastor's kid, I knew in my *brain* that God was always there for me, choosing and caring for me, but my heart still didn't believe it. I really didn't buy into the fact that there was Someone perfect in my life who always, *always* jumped up and down and cheered me on, no matter what life dished out. "I pick you! I choose you! You are My pearl of great price!"

Instead, what I bought into, for years and years, was the lie that somehow I *wasn't* enough. Can you relate?

I grew up in a loving family, but felt pretty unseen a lot of the time anyway. *Unseen* and *overlooked* are word cousins, related to each other but with their own distinct meanings. It's one thing to feel invisible sometimes and another to have that feeling verified by the rejections of this world. Because when we sustain those stiff kicks to the shins, emotionally speaking, the message is loud and clear: "You don't deserve to be chosen."

One cringeworthy story from my archives seemed to bear this out. I'm talking about the Fashion Show Fiasco of My Childhood.

When I, a sixth-grader, heard about a special fashion show being put on at a local department store, I wanted to party like it was 1999. I was crazy excited about the idea of being part of a real, live fashion show! It was a dream come true. I always liked to play "model" when we were playing make-believe "house" with our neighborhood friends. My older sister, a few other friends, and I would regularly play house and we always had to establish what our story was before we began. We'd pick out our baby dolls, name them things like "Sugar" and "Spice," and set up our "houses." Every single time, I went rogue.

"I am going to set these aside for a few minutes, because I want to be a mom and get a husband later," I would say, laying down my baby dolls (obviously, I thought husbands grew on trees). "I want to be a model first." The other mini mamas would keep rolling with their *As the House Turns* scenarios, and I would practice my catwalk down the hallway. So when I spotted that fashion show flyer, calling for local girls to try out, the whole thing had my name written all over it.

I remember my sweet mom's resistance. I could tell by her body language and face that she didn't really want to hassle with this. It wouldn't just involve me, because my sisters were sure to want to join in as well. But in the end she couldn't resist me on my knees, hands clasped together, begging her to make the call about the tryouts. "Yes," she said, "I'll call the number and see what this is all about." I was thrilled. This would be it! The beginning of my modeling career. Watch out, Heidi Klum. Step back, Tyra Banks! Ashley Reitz was coming to a runway near you!

Yeah—way off on that. Not only did the fashion show organizers not have room for me in their production, but they *did* have room for my sisters, you know, the ones who were always busy burping Sugar and Spice and asking their imaginary husbands what they wanted for dinner.

"Honey," my mom said, "they don't have room for you. You're not going to be able to participate." I can still see my mom's eyes when she broke the news to me. I bet it killed her to have to tell me that. Even now, I wonder if in her initial resistance she'd had a bad feeling about this fashion show.

I fumed until steam was blowing out my ears. I cried until my body ran out of water. But it was all no use. I hadn't been chosen. I had been overlooked. Worse, my sisters, to whom this didn't mean nearly as much, had been embraced and included. My heart was broken into smithereens like only a sensitive preteen girl's heart can be. The fashion show had meant everything to me. On a deeper level, the show symbolized my intense desire to be recognized as someone special in the eyes of others.

Oh, it was pretty bad—I'm not gonna lie. First there was the grueling time leading up to the fashion show, when my sisters and my neighbor girls (who had heard about it from me and who had also been selected to walk the runway) were excitedly chattering about the show—the extravagant luncheon they were going to beforehand, and the thank-you goodie bag they would each receive. Each rapturous comment was salt on my wound, and a reminder that I would be on the outside looking in. There was no place at this magical event for an average girl like me.

The dark day dawned and I watched as my sisters breathlessly drove off in their golden horse-drawn carriage and…All right, so it wasn't a horse-drawn carriage, but I sure did feel like Cinderella, left behind to scrub floors with a toothbrush. It wasn't even as if the household mice sang to me and collectively sewed a lustrous blue dress from my mother's tablecloth. No prince. No glass slipper. Just a sad, tearstained little moppet, flopped on her bed, feeling as if she had already turned into a chubby pumpkin.

My parents were gentle and loving to me; their support buoyed me up. I had so much more to be thankful for. But they couldn't fix this for me. They had taught me about Jesus, who comforts us when we feel left behind. But somehow I didn't make the connection between my heartbreak and Jesus's embracing, accepting love for me. I didn't realize on a soul level that my Father sat next to me on that pink ruffled bedspread in 1999. He saw me, noticed me, and cared about my bruised heart. He knew that I had been wounded by this rejection, and He hates it when His girls are hurt.

Of course, Jesus knew this wasn't the end of my story, not by a long shot. He knew the desires of my heart and my dreams of celebrating them, and He had in mind a major "plot twist" for my future, just as He has in mind a major plot twist for yours!

When was the last time you felt like Cinderella, left behind to scrub the floors instead of being swept up in something wonderful? Can you think of a time you felt kicked to life's curb? He sits next to you, longing for you to lean in and tell Him all about it. He longs to comfort you and fill you with His acceptance and favor. Do you believe it?

Unfortunately, I didn't believe it—yet. My fashion show wound festered for years, reinforcing my seemingly bottomless desire to do and be anything that resulted in validation and approval. As a teen, this need kicked into high gear. I worked double, triple overtime, trying, striving to be the kind of girl no one would ever overlook again. When I wasn't making every effort to be prettier and thinner, I pulled out all the stops to be more acceptable, more popular. Talk about a hamster wheel to nowhere! No matter how much effort I put in, that bad old world knocked me down again and again. And yet I kept slogging it out, trying to be accepted, included, embraced, and chosen.

Oh, how I wish I could travel back in time to my teen years and tell myself the truth—that I was included, embraced, and chosen, even though I didn't *feel* it.

During high school, there was one area in which I tried until the cows came home, and it didn't make one bit of difference: math. Math! Or more specifically, accounting class, circa 2007.

Let me back up a bit: You know how we often categorize ourselves as right-brained or left-brained? Left-brain functioning is usually characterized by those with analytical strengths—facts, order, numerals, and decimals.

The right brain is usually referenced for more creative, daydreaming, free-spirited types of personalities. I am definitely almost all right-brained. Of course, we all have a different mixture and makeup of the two types, but I am overwhelmingly a righty when it comes to my brain. God bless you lefties!

The way I am wired, I feel my most joyful and complete when I'm involved in splashing paint, listening to music, and creating something. Give me numbers to crunch or factoids to memorize and a little rash starts to develop on my arm.

This is where my teen years come in. The high school I attended seemed to be filled with academic rock stars who were obviously headed for PhDs, the Oval Office, or NASA. Motivated by my desire to fit in, I decided to take an accounting elective one year.

I am going to give everything I possibly can give to

this class, I told myself. And I did. I invested tons of time studying. I gave all the attention to that class I could possibly muster. But it wasn't enough. By the time the second semester rolled around I was living in a state of abject misery over this one class. Accounting was my dark night of the soul that year, and sadly I had to walk into it three times a week. Every time a test would be handed back, I felt like heaving. And sure enough, it seemed as if everyone around me was cooing at their test papers, glowing brightly with As, while my dim bulb could barely flicker out a C−. Ashamed and defeated, I would quickly fold my test in half so no one could see my terrible grade.

Lord, you forgot my smarts, I railed at God inwardly. *Any way we could get a refund on the left side of my brain? It doesn't seem to be operating properly.*

Again, what seemed effortless to others—or at least doable (i.e., to just be who they were and still be viewed as favorable and significant)—was way beyond my reach. With each C−, I would feel kicked to the curb again, deemed not good enough.

The worst part of that year wasn't even accounting class. The low point was the class debate, in which I was forced to participate. None of this "what happens in the classroom stays in the classroom" sensibility either. It was a *public* debate. Parents were invited. Stone-cold dread flooded me as I braced myself. This could not possibly end well.

As far as I could tell, my classmates were pumped up about it! Especially Sylvie Van Antwerp, the daughter of a lawyer, the smartest and meanest girl in school. Guess who I was paired with to debate? Sylvie thrived on humiliating others publicly. She poked fun at their background, what they wore, how they spoke, anything at all. She poked fun at *my* background, what I wore, how I spoke, anything at all! For me to debate Sylvie was like throwing a gladiator into the Colosseum with a bunny. An NBA player on the basketball court with a jockey.

Pretty much whatever horrible ending you are envisioning for me came true that day. Total humiliation, and I don't even have a T-shirt that says, "What doesn't kill you makes you stronger" or "Sylvie slaughtered me in the debate and all I got was this dumb shirt."

At the time, all I could see and feel was embarrassment. It really was the worst to work so hard in accounting and get Cs. It was even worse to be called out so publicly in that debate, shown up for all to see as an obvious dimwit.

We've all had experiences like this one. We've all had our own personal "dungeons," our own accounting class or math class or whatever it is. We've all felt totally overlooked while it seems as if everyone around us has been chosen and blessed. And we all have different areas of weakness that seem to trip us up on a regular basis.

Maybe you're like me and would rather be slapped in the face with a wet fish than take a math or accounting test.

Or perhaps you're the complete opposite, and your brain is wired to compute all those numbers and factoids with dizzying efficiency! You're a STEM phenom, but you are the last one picked for any athletic endeavor—and that includes Team Bass Fishing and Bowling. (I literally looked up the two sports that take the least athletic skill and found out there *is* Team Bass Fishing in some high schools!)

Perhaps you're a popular, pretty girl who has lots of friends but doesn't get the respect you would like at work.

There are endless variations on the same theme: I'm not good at _____ (fill in the blank) and it makes me feel really bad about myself. Or worse, I'm not as good as I *want* to be at something. It doesn't help when there's someone like Sylvie in the picture, always ready and waiting for her chance to take you down a peg or two. And there is always a Sylvie in the picture—can I get a witness?

You know how they say "Time heals all wounds"? I don't know about "all wounds," but time certainly gives a person perspective on old wounds. I look back at my teenage angst and see things with new clarity. I see how my anxiety was driven by a faulty engine to want *people* to accept and choose me. The key word there is people. I was searching and striving to somehow be good enough in a particular area to make those around me give me the acceptance and celebration I craved. How messed up was that? Have you ever strived to be "good enough" at something, for somebody?

Yes, it was merely human to be hurt and frustrated by my seeming inability to get a solid grade in a math-related class or to mount an effective rebuttal to Sylvie in the debate.

I wish I had handled things differently. It was okay to cry and feel upset about it all, but I wish I had spent lots of time in the comforting, wise presence of the One who heals all our wounds. Leaning on Him, praying for wisdom and courage and help—that's the way to get through it when someone rejects you. That's the way to grow from a hurtful experience, when life gives us the cold shoulder.

I see now that Jesus wired me a certain way—and that He loves the way He wired me! Creative, a dreamer—a righty!

That does *not* mean it would have been okay to slack off in accounting class. First Corinthians 15:58 says, "Throw yourselves into the work of the Master, confident that *nothing you do for him is a waste of time or effort*" (MSG, emphasis added). God wanted me to try my best, but not because I had a point to prove. Not because I was striving and struggling for some shred of affirmation and approval. Yeah, I was barking up the wrong tree for that!

Yet there is good news for you and me when we experience rejection. It's in those times, when we butt up against something hard and even impossible, over and over again, that an opportunity presents itself. A truly golden, shining opportunity. I'm talking about the chance to be comforted and loved by Love. When we are overlooked, we can turn to the One who accepts us and chooses us and change our outlook. We see the situation through eyes of Love, not through our own flawed vision. We are reminded of our worth and value and how loved we are. We are told again that our wiring— whether for numbers or paint or animals or whatever it is that makes us *us*—is not only pleasing to God but delightful. Did you get that, friend? Your wiring— whether for numbers or paint or animals or whatever it is that makes you *you*—pleases and delights God!

Because He wastes nothing, our Father takes our

pain and converts it to new and beautiful things—
compassion and empathy for others and a renewed vision for our place in God's kingdom. In other words,
Jesus turns the ashes of rejection into something useful
and good.

Sometimes, waiting for something we want—for
someone to look our way and choose us—is the hardest piece of being overlooked. I know I can feel the
most unwanted when I am "waiting my turn" for
something, especially when it's something everyone
around me seems to be getting.

For me, the biggest area is my ringless left ring
finger. I definitely feel a little bit shunned in the relationship department. Oh, it's partly my fault—I'm
fully aware that I've taken a very different approach to
relationships than most in the world. I wanted to date
differently because I really believed in dating for marriage. My friends and I used to joke around and say
"no recreational dating" for me. I genuinely wanted
to—and still want to—find the guy I'll be with forever.
My attitude about this was terrific when I was eighteen, and then nineteen, and then twenty. But around
the age of twenty-one, I started to think I might need
to put a little note in God's suggestion box: *Hey, Lord!
Yoo-hoo! Remember me? Nice little church girl Ashley
with the heart for You? Don't You know any suitable
gents You could pivot in my general direction?*

Coming from a traditional area of the Midwest, it
appeared to me as if every single girl was in love and
planning her happily-ever-after. Yes, at the age of
twenty-one! If you hit twenty-three with no ring in
sight you start to sweat, and your collection of brides-
maid dresses begins to dominate your closet.

For most of my early twenties, I thought if I was obedient, prayed diligently, trusted emphatically, surely the right guy would just appear the next time I went grocery shopping. Just like a cheesy Hallmark movie, we would probably reach for the same kumquat at the same time and then boom—love at first sight in Aisle Six!

My happily-ever-after has just not happened. Year after year, for the most part, I have remained "on the shelf," or at least that's what it feels like. And it's getting a little old.

Waiting my turn while my friends have gotten engaged or married has been rough. I mean, if I was sitting on the shelf like a well-preserved bakery item along with all my friends, that would be a different story. I would have shelf company! But no, it seems as if friends and acquaintances have flown *off* the shelf. In demand. Wanted. Chosen. All the single ladies around me seem to be chosen by someone. And after a few years of this, I started to feel pretty lonely. If no one wanted me, after all my hopes and dreams, did it mean I wasn't worth as much as those around me? The question plagues me sometimes, in my weakest moments.

You know what makes it so much worse, this business of being overlooked? Social media. A simple scroll through my phone might reveal…

- A pal's Instagram posts of a dazzling diamond ring, proof that someone wanted to "wife them up."
- A cousin's tweet about how drinking coffee with their sweetie is better than drinking it alone.

- A former classmate's Facebook post featuring a photo of his-and-hers monogrammed towels hanging in the bathroom.

Ugh! Some days I want to throw my phone out the window. On those hard days when I really want to drink coffee with someone cute, or shop for matchy monogrammed towels, those carefully curated shots of my social media friends' lives can make me feel even lonelier and more inadequate. Unless you live in a cave somewhere, you can likely relate. We get ourselves into trouble when we take our eyes off our own paths and look over at someone else's.

Writer Jennifer Garam, in an article for *Psychology Today* called "Social Media Makes Me Feel Bad About Myself," is so right when she talks about what happens when we linger in our social media feeds:[2]

I immediately get sucked into comparing and despairing, and lose all sense of groundedness, of being anchored to my life. Untethered, I float away from my ability to feel good about myself and my accomplishments.

She nails it, right? Social media, like so many other good things, is helpful and fun in moderation. Yet when we buy into our friends' *seemingly* perfect, oppressively cheerful lives without taking into consideration that no one is that happy all the time, we drift off from what is real and true. It can be downright toxic when we "float away" from the truth of our worth, into the smog of Cyber La La Land and all of its lies. Because the truth is, social media is a highlight reel, the icing on someone's cake! No one posts about their Friday night alone, licking chip crumbs out of the bag. Or their anxious thoughts and feelings that they, too, feel overlooked and lonely.

The answer is not to throw our phone out the window and shut down our social media accounts. But regular breaks are a good idea. Obviously, when we see something online that triggers thoughts of not measuring up, we have to get off immediately. It's poison to see all the shiny, happy people at parties you haven't been invited to or enjoying some status or favor you long to enjoy. And why—*why?*—would we willingly breathe in poison?

You may not have been invited to the party or on the date or into the "inner circle"—whatever being chosen might look like for you—but you have been invited to something wonderful, something of far greater value.

When you feel overlooked, it's another chance to deepen your relationship with Someone who chooses you every time. For you, for me, it's here, in our heart of hearts, where God lives, that we breathe in fresh, bracing oxygen and we are grounded in our identities as the Father's cherished daughters. Here we are established and formed, built up and set free. Teresa of Avila called this sacred space an "interior castle," and here we listen as the King tells us we are:

- Handpicked
- Exceptional
- Distinctive
- And so Dearly Loved

The fact that God chooses us changes everything!

When we are uninvited and passed over by a selfish, cracked world, we can go to Him who is always near, including us and celebrating us just the way we are (no filter).

He claps for us when we try and try and still get a bad grade.

He cheers us on when others beat us down.

He cherishes us when we feel at our least attractive and desirable, when it seems as if everyone has turned their backs on us.

In our loneliness and heartbreak, He is our Companion and Healer. He simply never rejects His girls, for whom He died. Never. No matter what. And when people make us feel like we are on the outside looking in, shunned, and scorned, we can be sure Jesus understands.

Our Comforter was bruised and rejected His whole life:

- As a child, Jesus was thought to be illegitimate. He was poor, a refugee from Herod, and later a lowly carpenter's son in a tacky small town.
- Jesus was misunderstood by His parents, His friends, the people of His hometown, who thought He was crazy and even demon-possessed.
- When things really got tough for Jesus, His closest friends deserted Him. One even denied knowing Him. "Then all the disciples forsook him, and fled" (Matt. 26:56 KJV).
- At the end of His life, Jesus was ridiculed, falsely accused, beaten, tortured, and crucified, His beautiful life thrown away like garbage.

He understands what it is to be overlooked. No matter how coldly we've been rejected, or how overwhelmingly we've been snubbed, we can find hope and strength in the God who gets it—and gets us. We can never fall through the cracks on His watch—He's perfect; there are no cracks!

You are beautiful! When the world says, "You're not enough," God is waiting for His chance to set you straight. "You are enough, My pearl of great price. I know, because I made you enough. I will never overlook you, on this earth and for all of eternity."

Beauty Box

1. Think of two examples of times in your life when you felt snubbed, rejected, and overlooked. Write them down in a notebook, and say the following prayer over these memories: *Jesus, it hurt like crazy when I was rejected by that person or through that situation. Because You are the Father who heals, I ask for Your healing and grace as a balm and relief to my wound. I ask that You show me that person or that situation through Your eyes, and help me forgive them for hurting me.*

2. God wired you in a completely one-of-a-kind, singular, delightful way! Write down five areas of "wiring" or strengths in your life and thank God for giving you those gifts!

3. Consider this: "Jesus knew that I had been wounded by this rejection, and He hates it when His girls are hurt." Do you believe this to be true when *you* are hurt?

4. I confess that in high school, I put too much pressure on myself in accounting class to win the acceptance I craved from those around me. Have you ever strived to be "good enough" at something, for somebody?

5. "You may not have been invited to the party or on the date or into the 'inner circle'—whatever being chosen might look like for you…" What does being chosen look like for you?

6. When you're constantly hit with social media posts that show only happy moments in people's lives, it's easy to think yours isn't good enough. Social me-

dia shouldn't make you feel inadequate, and if it is, make that your cue to log off.

7. Open up to a trusted friend about feeling overlooked. Invite her to open up to you, and promise to pray for her and encourage her!

3
PRETTY

Do you remember your first encounter with beauty products? Maybe your aunt bought you a tinted lip balm when you were eleven, or you and your bestie did makeovers on each other with her big sister's stash of blush and eyeshadow.

I blame my Nana. That woman started me young in the lipstick aisle! Every time we would visit she would bring out these bulging ziplock bags of makeup and nail polish, and my sisters and I would fight over which ones we wanted. My mom was never very much into makeup, but I could always count on Nana. One of my favorite things to this day is to browse the aisles of makeup while shopping with my beloved, un-frumpy grandmother.

For me, using makeup and hair products were about a lot of different things. I was hooked on beauty from the very first time I sat my little fifth-grade booty down for my first chemical hair-straightening treatment. I just knew that someday I, too, would learn how to make other girls' beauty dreams come true. I would try anything that was supposed to make me look pretty. I mimicked any trend I saw older girls doing, even white eyeliner! Do you remember that? Such a weird trend, and it made us all look like White Eyelash Vipers. And speaking of eyeliner, a few years later I spent my whole senior trip bus ride down to Florida teaching my classmates, teachers, and chaperones how to perfect winged liquid eyeliner (which made us all look like Cleopatra, a big improvement!).

I went to private school with many girls whose families were well-off financially, and I knew I couldn't keep up with the way they dressed or all the things they had. I was well aware that I wasn't the prettiest girl in the class and wasn't the one that all the boys were after. But I tried so hard to do what I could to make myself feel pretty, to be wanted, to be seen as enough. Yet every day the only thing I knew was that I would never be pretty enough.

The truth is, none of us will ever be pretty enough! We all want to feel beautiful, to be wanted, to be thought of as good-looking. It's something innate in each one of us, and something with which we have to come to terms.

I've already laid out in detail the way I was the chubby one in the middle of two ballerinaesque sisters. Not only was I the bigger girl in my family, I was also less pretty than my sisters, or at least that's the way I perceived things.

"Oh, look at how darling Andrea and Lauren are in their Easter dresses!" Relatives and church members would cluck and fuss over the *other* Reitz girls. And then they would invariably notice me, big eyes pricking with unshed tears, noticing, observing, and storing their comments away in my inner vault. "Oh, and you too, Ashley! Aren't you sweet as well." Whatever. Like I bought *that*. We need to give kids more credit. They're sharp, keenly perceptive, always on the alert for how they think others see them. *Do people see me as appealing and attractive or unappealing and unattractive?* We instinctively want to know these things at a tender age.

Forging peace with our looks is a lifelong process, which starts in childhood and gets very dicey in middle school. At least for me, middle school didn't help one bit. Those three years left me with boatloads of insecurity, on a constant search to figure out how to be prettier, how to become worthy of love and admiration.

By the time I was in ninth grade, I had a strong drive to be lovelier in the eyes of my peers and important grown-ups. I had made it my full-time job during the summer and school breaks to make sure that I was doing everything I possibly could to be seen as prettier. I read every single *Seventeen* magazine I could get my hands on. If there was a tip on how to wear an eyeshadow to contour your eye shape and flatter your eye color, I was in. I was going to highlight, tan, paint, and fake bake my way to being the most adorable person I could be. (Yes, the dreaded "fake bake." I would tan in tanning beds and then glop sunless tanning lotion all over if I thought the color achieved wasn't dark enough. But I did usually stop just shy of morphing into a human orange baboon, in case you're wondering.)

So I brushed and blushed and contoured and applied and highlighted and glopped—I executed all the pretty-making maneuvers for the desired result: Prettiness. But it wasn't all bad. Even though my core reason for all this eyeliner, lip gloss, and foundation was negative—I was trying to fix what I was feeling inside—a love for beauty and beauty products can be positive.

I really want you to know that so I will say it again, in all caps:

A LOVE FOR BEAUTY AND BEAUTY PRODUCTS CAN BE POSITIVE!

God has given us the desire to feel desired, and it's natural to want to feel pulled together, to play up our God-given features and just plain have fun with the stuff! For me, new brushes and shades of eye color and lip color and nail color make me swoon. They are my toys! I genuinely have a blast using different combinations of products to create matchless looks. For me, it's a hoot and a half to help a friend achieve a really lovely look for a special night out.

Some days I want to go completely natural and clean, and other days there might be an out-of-the-ordinary event and I want to glam it up with eyeliner and bold colors. I no longer feel guilty, as I once did.

Were you, like me, born with a longing for beauty? Whether it's a gorgeous flower garden or a new lip color, many of us are drawn magnetically to those things. Personally, I have never met a tube of lip color I didn't want to try! Well, maybe I didn't want to try Irish Green or Mellow Yellow. Ain't no girl who can pull those off!

There has to be a balance, though. We do need to always keep our hearts in check. Are we using these products in hopes that they will make us feel good or feel good enough? There's a big difference. The truth is, no beauty treatment known to womankind can confer deep value to the secret places in our souls. Only Jesus can do that. Do you believe it?

It's interesting, how the conversation about beauty changes in and out of the church setting. What does a good Christian girl look like? Does she wear no makeup? Does she wear only skirts to the floor? Does she have blue streaks in her hair and a nose piercing? The answer is yes. Yes. And yes! We all have different convictions and are at different points in our lives. As long as our choices and hearts seek to honor God with what we choose and how we portray ourselves, then I don't care if you are bohemian natural, edgy with the side of your head shaved, Sporty Spice with your hair in a ponytail, or wearing stilettos and a designer dress. You be you!

When I was younger I didn't always feel this way. Some of my most insecure moments related to my appearance were in church. Have you ever felt that way? I somehow believed I had to look a certain way, act a certain way, and hide my personality inside the walls of my church. How I craved the confidence and security to just be me! My dad was the pastor, and he loved me to pieces. But I often felt that not all his congregants loved the way I presented myself. My hair color changed—often. I favored bright reds and pinks and blues and greens on my nails, and animal prints on my blouses, my dresses, my shoes, my purses...I was like a cheetah on the loose in those days.

Honestly, I felt like I would have been more accepted if I dressed like an Amish girl.

Mind you, everything I wore was modest and appropriate in terms of coverage. There were no short skirts or low-cut tops—not on my mother's watch! And not on my watch either. I truly had the desire to be a "good Christian girl." So it was confusing and intimidating to me that I was just trying to be me—Ashley the girl, not Ashley the PK. Somehow my zippy, colorful, cheetah-printed, blush-loving persona was found wanting, and it hurt.

You see, the girls at my church were fairly plain in style, but I was ultra girly. One time, I wore my hair up in a high poof, not quite like Snookie of *Jersey Shore* fame, but not far off either. Someone said, "What are you hiding in there?" *Hardy har har.*

I'll never forget walking into church and seeing a group of young people in a circle. They were talking, and when one person said something they all turned and looked at me. I didn't know exactly why these kids were talking about me, but it stung. I had moved while in my freshman year of high school to this new town and church, and clearly I did not fit in. When in your life have you felt as if you didn't fit in?

By the time I was a junior in high school, I sensed I was coming into my own. I was slowly growing more comfortable with who I was. Or so I thought. I was looking to create who I was going to become as a young adult. I was known among my friends as the beauty maven of Adrian, Michigan. Ha! Maybe not. But I spent money from my barista job to get my hair and nails done. I liked the way I was, and except for when someone gave me the stink-eye in the church foyer for wearing toenail polish in an un-approved shade of Iniquity Red, I didn't care what anyone else thought. Until one day I was put on the spot by a Bible study group leader.

I looked up to this young woman, a guest leader for our high school girls' Bible study. When you're seventeen, you think twenty-five-year-olds are pretty cool. She seemed to have it all down. She had gone to college, had a great love story with her perfect Christian boyfriend, and gave the impression of knowing a thing or two about faith and life. I soaked up what she said whenever she made an appearance to lead the group.

One day, she brought up the topic of makeup. "I used to love wearing makeup and going glam in my younger years, but no longer," she said. "I now believe I wore makeup as a mask to cover up my insecurities." My heart dropped. She went on, insinuating that those who did wear makeup were trying to play a part, that they were not being themselves. She hinted that makeup wearers were unhappy with themselves if they chose to alter what God had given them. I was the obvious target in the room, and I felt pierced by her pointed words. *She thinks less of me because of my thick mascara and acrylic nails*, I thought. And I went straight to shame, as we women so often do. From my perceived impression of my Bible study leader's poor impression of me, I extrapolated that *everyone* thought less of me because of my thick mascara and acrylic nails! When you believe everyone thinks you are lacking, it's only a tiny step to believing you *are* lacking. Do the math with me:

A: (Someone whose opinion matters) thinks I am (ugly, silly, boring, dumb, not spiritual enough…)

B: Therefore all his/her friends and relatives and acquaintances and somehow everyone in the universe must also think I am (ugly, silly, boring, dumb, not spiritual enough…)

Thus, A + B = C: I *am* (ugly, silly, boring, dumb,
   not spiritual enough...)!

Hey, I know it doesn't make any sense, but in our
fallen state, our thought processes can be pretty
messed up. Remember we talked about the power of
self-talk in chapter 1? It's crucial that we check ourselves at this point, when we start to believe the lies
about our worth. We have to catch ourselves thinking
this way, and spend time with the One who transforms
our self-talk. For instance, I could have said, back
in the day, to my bruised self, something like this:
"Ash, just because your Bible study leader seems to
think you are not spiritual enough because you love to
wear makeup does not make it true. The truth is, God
knows your heart. He loves your creativity and flair.
And when He sees you, He sees beauty, fun, sparkle,
and a heart that leans toward Him in the most pleasing
way."

I wish I had given myself that little talk, but I didn't.
Oh no, I went headlong in the wrong direction, striving to "self-correct" and do better, *be better*, in order
to become that good Christian girl I so wanted to be.

For a time, I tried wearing less makeup to see if I
discovered a whole new, super-spiritual part of me that
I didn't know existed. Maybe I would discover that
cosmetics were as evil as my Bible study made them
out to be!

At first I just slowly toned down the makeup. I
wanted in my heart of hearts to be a "good Christian
girl." (There's that description again!) And if wearing
makeup wasn't a part of that, then I'd eventually get
rid of it. I decided to wean myself off, and one day

I was ready. "I'm confident enough to wear zero makeup to school today," I told my sister.

The very first class in the morning, during prayer requests, my teacher pointed to me. "Ashley, are you feeling okay? You look a little peaked." Naturally every student swiveled around in their seats to examine my naked, sickly face. I was slightly mortified, but not as embarrassed as I would have thought. Realizing I could embody a "who cares?" attitude, I decided to run with it—the attitude, not the guilt for wearing makeup. I decided I was the same Ashley with or without makeup. Although I don't agree with the slant my Bible study leader had taken, that makeup was somehow inherently bad, I needed to find a balance between using it as a mask and simply enjoying it for what it was.

For me, it was a pivotal challenge. I learned to say "to each her own." I understood that, as far as makeup and beauty products went, there was no right or wrong as long as my heart was in the right place and my intentions were to please God with my appearance. Of course, my heart was often in the wrong place. I still fell into hoping that a beauty product would finally make me feel wanted, accepted, and worthy of attention. That feeling was something I would wrestle with for years before I figured it out.

My makeup-free phase was ten years ago. Times have changed, and not always in good ways. Now the beauty industry plays an even more whopping role in our lives. Ten years ago, social media wasn't nearly as popular or widely used as it is today. Facebook was becoming the hot thing back then. Now we have

Facebook and all its social media sisters, including Instagram. Ah, Instagram! No other social media platform to date showcases our desire to be beautiful like Insta does.

I love it, but I hate it too. It can be so unreal. We compare our actual, tangible, ever-changing daily lives to staged photos, carefully planned, in some cases by professionals, photoshopped by software, covered in filters, and paired with written posts that are nearly as fake. I'm as guilty as the next gal for getting sucked into the comparison trap. I look at lifestyle bloggers and think, *Wow, what an amazingly perfect life. Must be nice.*

We see a blog post about a new recipe for blueberry pie, featuring a photo of a beautiful, thin woman with an adorable baby on her hip. She is holding a pretty white plate with scalloped edges, bearing a juicy piece of pie. It's sunset in her universe, and layers of pink and peach sky frame the shot. My word—look at her ring! (Quick! Think of the last time you were jealous of someone's perfect life on social media. If you're like most of us, it was probably about an hour ago or less.)

Here's the thing: We too often forget that before that photo, Pie Polly may have stayed in her jammies baking and making a mess in the kitchen, stopping frequently to change her baby's poopy diapers. (Gasp, that precious child from the photo poops?!) When her husband got home from work, she quickly threw on a different outfit, carefully cut a perfect wedge of pie and asked her husband—who was slightly grumpy from a long day at work—to try to capture the flawless photo for her blog. We see only a one-second snap of a very long, sweaty, exasperating day, but the reality part is left out. This leaves us with a false example of what we *should* be, somehow, if only we tried harder. This is the goal many of us are trying to achieve. And it's ruining us.

Studies show that girls and young women are exposed to 10.4 hours a day of perfect images to live up to. There's Instagram, and then there's the beauty bloggers and vloggers. The top YouTube beauty vloggers run from 3 to 10 million regular subscribers, not including the millions more who simply watch the videos. I have definitely sat and watched a girl from another country show me her daily makeup routine simply because I want to know how to re-create the look for myself. These girls—beauty vloggers—have millions upon millions of views per video and make that their full-time job. I am not alone in being a sucker for that stuff.

Ten years ago, I just flipped through magazines here and there. Magazines can be bad enough. I recently saw a headline in a teen beauty magazine that read, "Wake up pretty!" Like that's an achievable goal! But now we also have social media and a massive online beauty industry.

Don't get me wrong—I'm not condemning the beauty industry! I just told you I was a pushover for all that jazz. But again, we have to be watchful. Are we getting caught up in the impossible desire to be worthy? Are we buying into the media's ever-blasting message—that to be prettier is to be more valuable? Do we think we have to keep up with the vloggers and bloggers, for fear that if we don't we will somehow be found wanting even more?

Let's not get swept up in lies that we are only worthy, lovable, and acceptable if we somehow match up to the media's narrow definition of beauty. It's like walking a tightrope—constricted, ridiculous, and dangerous to our hearts. Because the truth is, we will never be pretty enough. No one will be.

How do we fight the lies? How do we find the true source of our purpose, worth, and love? Time for a major mind shift.

Let's take a minute to contemplate the *Real Housewives of* _____ (insert a city). I call these types of shows "Gorgeous Women Behaving Badly." Millions of viewers tune in to these shows for their fix of feistiness—or fight-i-ness. We sure don't DVR shows with names such as *Average-Looking Women with Inner Beauty Being Grace-Bearers*. It's human nature to want to see the screeching, the scheming, the clawing, and the bleeding too. We even want to see shows about animals behaving badly (cue up *My Cat from Hell*. Notice there's no show called *My Placid Pet Purring in a Patch of Sunlight*). We crave the drama, baby!

These women spend fortunes on hair, makeup, cosmetic surgery, and personal trainers to look incredible, yet the way they treat each other can be downright *hideous*. Their extreme emphasis on outward appearance at the expense of inner beauty—strength, kindness, and love—epitomizes how messed up our culture is these days! Think of how we unconsciously buy into the message: If you look pretty, it doesn't matter how you treat others or behave when no one else is looking.

It's the opposite of God's values!

Two thousand years ago, it was this excessive focus on outer beauty that prompted the apostle Peter to write the following to his church members: "Your beauty should not come from outward adornment, such as elaborate hairstyles and the wearing of gold jewelry or fine clothes. Rather, it should be that of your inner self, the *unfading beauty* of a gentle and quiet spirit, which is of great worth in God's sight" (1 Pet. 3:3–4, emphasis added).

His readers were a community of married women who were new to following Christ. These women were rich and fabulous, kind of like our friends from the *Real Housewives*. Peter's new disciples were steeped in their beauty-idolizing sophisticated culture like teabags in hot water. They vied against each other for the best hair, makeup, and jewelry-using techniques. They spent lots of money. Loads of time. Tons of energy. All that effort was devoted to the pursuit of beauty, and the desire to be *pretty enough*. Like many of us, these women wanted to be admired and wanted by all who saw them. Sound familiar?

Get this: Peter isn't telling his glam church ladies to quit with the kohl and banish the balsam oil. Instead, he was asking them to check their hearts, to aspire to *more* than being the glitziest housewife Asia Minor had ever seen, to *more* than being prettier than their neighbor.

"Peter isn't being harsh when he speaks to the women," says author and blogger Barb Roose. "He wasn't bashing beauty enhancements; rather, he contrasts what a woman does with her outer appearance against what God accomplishes by His divine work within us."[3]

"Your beauty should…come from…your inner self." These verses teach us that our appearance has nothing to do with our worth. Getting pretty may be a fun perk to being a girl, but prettiness on its own holds no value. A pretty spirit? Now that's worth something! Next time we feel carried away with the too-hot pursuit of prettiness, we need to stop and press reset. How can we prioritize inner beauty over outer in a world that screams "pretty, pretty, pretty"?

Peter's words are ageless, cutting across two millennia of time. They were for the Real Housewives of Cappadocia and they are for us today. He calls every holy daughter to make sure that God-cultivated, flourishing inner beauty is most important.

It's the kind of beauty that blossoms, prospers, and glows brighter even as our outward prettiness shrivels, decreases, and dims. Carrie Fisher tweeted once, when she was attacked for her looks, "Please stop debating about whether or not I aged well. Youth and beauty are not accomplishments, they're the temporary, happy by-products of time and/or DNA." Princess Leia speaks truth! Like King Solomon wrote in Proverbs 31:30, "Beauty is fleeting; but a woman who fears the LORD is to be praised."

In other words, pretty is as pretty does. We are only as beautiful as the way we treat others, only as pretty as our behavior and actions. Are we, as Peter exhorted the women of the early church, spending time cultivating the true accomplishments of being gracious, friendly, and humble? Are we choosing to possess God's peace and trust Him as opposed to living in and acting out of fear? This is what Peter means by "quiet" and "gentle." Instead of "quiet," think "peaceable," and instead of "gentle," think "kindhearted." You talkative, exuberant girls out there need not worry: You don't have to undergo a personality trans-plant to nurture inner beauty!

To be a pretty-does girl means we have to heal from the inside out. We have to saturate our minds with the truth that God adores us, no matter if all the world sees is our acne and our wiry hair and our lumpy thighs. To Him who gave His child to save you and me, to set us free, each one of us is beautiful beyond description.

He's crazy about you!

He's wild about me!

He sees us as lovely, captivating, adorable, just the way we are, big or small, pretty or not by the world's standards. There is no way that you or I could ever become more valuable to Him than we are at this very moment. Your value is priceless now, not when you get your hair done and your makeup looks especially fetching.

God always views each one of us as a masterpiece. You are His work of art, His stroke of genius! The more time we spend with Him, listening to Him, praising Him, and learning about Him, the more we will believe where our worth comes from, where our confidence and wholeness comes from. It's okay to want to feel pretty, to enjoy the pursuit of prettiness, but we have to remember beauty is fleeting, aka short-lived! It's okay to "get into" beauty and even have it be our hobby, as long as it's not our obsession. Because why would we be obsessed with something that won't last, when we could be fascinated with something that will last forever?

We can try, try, try to be the prettiest or even mar-ginally prettier, but end up where we started—empty and frustrated. Only Jesus can fill those hollow places. We must stand on the solid, immovable realization that we are complete as is. *As is.* We are lovable by way of His love. We are enough because He made us so, giving us abundance from an overflowing cup. The beauty He gives His girls can never disappear.

Pretty or not, here He comes, with arms open wide to enfold us as His own perfect daughters. Isn't it time we finally believed this truth?

Beauty Box

1. Let's be on the ball next time we talk to a child in our lives. Are we focusing on their looks (and is someone else, who may not be as attractive, listening in)? Try and focus on a child's sense of humor, her intelligence, her insightful comments instead of her curls or cute outfit. And do dial up the sensitivity to who might be feeling overlooked.

2. "It's interesting, how the conversation about beauty changes in and out of the church setting." Does this resonate with you? What messages about beauty did you receive from the church? How are they different from the beauty messages you receive from Instagram or *Marie Claire*?

3. According to *Allure* magazine, nearly one third of millennials will do something unhealthy—smoke, tan, crash diet—if they think it will make them look better, while just 23 percent of Generation Xers and 16 percent of baby boomers will. This statistic shows how much more pretty-obsessed our generation is than the ones before. Also, 41 percent of millennials have felt better about themselves because someone else looked bad. (Only 28 percent of Generation X and 20 percent of baby boomers said they felt this way!) What do you think of this statistic? Next time you're tempted to feel better about yourself because someone else looks bad, tweak your thoughts instead. *Girl, that sister over there may be having a bad hair day, but she is a beloved image bearer of God*

Almighty! Then give her a word of encouragement, because, it's a bad hair day!⁴

4. I felt judged by the girls at church for being "too" interested in makeup and beauty products. Have you ever felt judged for wearing "too much" makeup? Maybe you felt judged for not wearing enough makeup?

5. How can you prioritize inner beauty over outer in a world that screams "pretty, pretty, pretty"?

6. "He sees us as lovely, captivating, adorable, just the way we are, big or small, pretty or not by the world's standards. There is no way that you or I could ever become more valuable to Him than we are at this very moment." Next time you have a hard time believing this is true, read these two passages:

   - "You are beautiful, for you are "fearfully and wonderfully made" (Ps. 139:14).
   - "You are altogether beautiful, my darling, beautiful in every way" (Song of Sol. 4:7 NLT).

4
SKINNY

What I noticed most about her was how loved she was, not how much she weighed.

I couldn't help myself. My eyes flitted from table to table and between two vastly different father-daughter scenarios. At one table in the coffee shop sat a little girl and her dad, talking. At the other table sat another little girl and her dad, not talking, except when the girl would try to get her dad's attention. Both girls were about the same age—eight or nine—and both dads were also similar in vintage. But what I witnessed at the table closer to me was a far cry from what I witnessed at the other table. I could tell just by observing that the two relationships were light-years apart in terms of closeness and connection.

The girl with little brown curls falling out of her ponytail had beautiful, sparkling brown eyes, chubby cheeks, rotund arms, and a round tummy that bulged out at the buttons of her blue cardigan. Bits of scone crumbs dusted her tummy. She had her father's rapt attention, as he smiled at her encouragingly, leaning in on his elbows to listen closer to her every utterance. At one point, she said something funny, I guess, because they both laughed. His listening posture was extraordinary—total engagement. Everything she said was so important to him. His eyes did not leave hers and he seemed so enthralled to be there sharing a scone with his daughter it was hard to imagine him wanting to be anywhere else.

Tears pricked my eyes. *How long had it been since someone leaned in like that to listen to me?* I thought. And then I realized my Father listens to me like that all day long, every day, and will never stop. *What a lovely portrait of God's love for His girls!* I thought, and decided to stop staring at them lest they think I was rude. *Who is that cuckoo woman staring at us, crying? Do we know her?*

My eyes shifted to the other table, the one to my right, which held another father-daughter pair. This little girl was petite with shiny blonde hair and so cute that had a Hollywood casting agent spotted her that day she would have been cast in a sitcom or movie. Blue eyes. Lashes for days. Sweet button of a nose. Unfortunately, her father seemed to be indifferent to her. He stared at his phone almost continuously, unless his daughter was trying to get his attention, which seemed to be every other minute. "Hey, Dad! Check this out!" She would have to repeat herself a couple of times before his eyes would flick toward her from his phone. "Yeah, okay, hon, just a sec…" And then he would dive back down the iPhone tunnel to his newsfeed, his texts, his world. His girl's shoulders finally slumped as she got lost in her own phone world, and they didn't speak to each other until it was time to go.

Two little girls. One who would in large part be defined by her extra weight, and the other who would find easy acceptance in most circles because of her dainty beauty. Both girls were at risk in a thin-obsessed world, but for different reasons. The brown-haired girl would be judged and maybe even bullied for her weight, yet because of her father's love for her, I was hopeful she could skip the self-loathing part and build on that self-love, nurtured by an extraordinarily attentive parent. I was more worried about the blondie. I mean, obviously, I was just observing one snapshot of their life. Every parent looks at their phone. Who knows? Maybe when they went home the two of them played Candyland for three hours before having a tea party with the stuffed hedgehog. But there was something lonely about her, as if she was used to being ignored.

I don't know what she was thinking, but I imagined her thoughts: *My looks will rescue me from feelings of insecurity. My looks will assure me a happy life. My looks promise me that I will always have love.*

Those beliefs were probably subconscious, but that kind of thinking—promoted in every crevice of our culture—is poison. The bigger girl could fight feelings of unworthiness because of her size, but the smaller girl could have just as much of a struggle—in some ways, worse. The pressure of having perfect teeth, skin, hair, and bodies will never go away unless she releases it to the One who says:

"*I* will rescue you from feelings of insecurity. *I* will assure you peace and joy. *I* promise you will always have love."

If only girls of all ages believed it! Because so often we don't believe our Father's truth, do we? Instead, we believe the messaging of our culture.

Tragically, the burden to be thin starts young. According to one study 42 percent of girls in first through third grades want to be thinner (Yeesh. They are *babies*!). Eighty-one percent of ten-year-olds are afraid of being fat!

How do we fight against all the voices in our culture that tell us that value is attached to being a certain size? How do we release ourselves from the terrible, toxic, stressful idea that one's worth is dependent on the number on the scale? Why have we gotten to a place in our society where we're only taught to care about how our bodies *look* rather than *feel*?

Sometimes we have to go back to go forward. We develop disordered thinking about our bodies from an impressionable age. What were we taught about our bodies and looks as children? Were you encouraged to respect and care for your own body, or treat it any which way in order to achieve a certain look?

Even as far back as fourth grade, I wanted to be wafer thin like my older sister and her friends, some of whom subsisted on a few apples per day. I didn't see their unhealthiness, only their desirable skinny frames, lean limbs, and fragile cheekbones. That's about the time that I started gaining weight, which led to frustration and feelings of self-loathing. Swimming lessons at school kicked off a whole new level of self-consciousness. How could I ever be as thin as I "should" be?

I wish that someone had come alongside me to redirect me from the futile pursuit of skinniness toward fullness and abundance—the truth that I was already special and valuable just as I was, chubby cheeks, round belly, and all. I had a hole inside that needed filling. The only problem was, I had no idea what to fill it with.

By the time I was a teenager, I was obsessed with off-loading my perceived heaviness, and it became normal for me to treat my body badly in the name of losing weight. I listened to the hiss in my ear telling me I wouldn't be lovable or wanted until I achieved the perfect body type. I struggled with the feeling that my size would determine my future. Teens are excessively hard on themselves, especially when it comes to their appearance, because they believe their image will determine a good outcome or a bad outcome. As we get older we understand that there is much more to life than size 6 jeans. We see the skinny, cool, popular kids graduate and many of them don't flourish the way it would seem they "should," given their "ideal body weight"! We also witness the kids with forty extra pounds, who may have been the most wilted of wallflowers in school, bloom into incredible, successful people. When you gain the golden perspective of being on the other side, you realize that the playing field is leveled.

But first you have to get *through* middle school and then high school! If only most of us could skip the unbearable pressure to be thin, the unnecessary stress to fit an impossible mold. I just know that like so many other teenage girls, I longed to be accepted, liked, and if I was lucky, adored.

At the age of twelve, I began paying my older sister to go get me diet pills at the store because I was too young to get them. "I don't care if the diet pills come with warnings or can cause damage," I told her. "I'd rather chance that than be fat."

I would have rather risked a cardiac event, hallucinations, "personality changes," or even death rather than be fat? Well, no one put it to me that way, but I honestly don't know if I would have cared. "Personality changes"? Who cares, as long as the old bod changes too! My mantra was "I don't care what I have to do to get a more desirable body."

So I did. I popped the diet pills, severely restricted what I ate, and exercised to an extreme degree, especially if I was feeling guilty about eating something "bad." The yo-yo dieting was an endless roller coaster. I would eat barely anything until I couldn't handle the hunger, and then of course I binged on everything edible. Defeated and ashamed, I would throw in the towel on my diet and eat tons of food until I once again felt pressure to go back to the apples.

If I felt shame about eating something unhealthy, I would sometimes force myself to that porcelain bowl, stick my fingers down my throat and get rid of it. Or if I couldn't purge myself for some reason I'd say "back to the gym" as a punishment. And that's what it was: a punishment, a penalty for not having the "self-control" to starve my body. Once, in my early twenties, I had worked out and was so famished on the way home I stopped at the drive-through and got a burger and fries. After I got home I felt so ashamed because I had "ruined" my workout, it drove me to the bathroom to "backtrack" what I had just done. *How sad*, I thought, as I washed my face and looked in the mirror with shame. *How unhealthy am I to do this?* I begged God for forgiveness and vowed to never purposely throw up my food again.

When I look back now at those times when I abused my body for the sake of skinniness, it grieves me. The self-disgust, loathing, and shame are simply on another level of low. And talk about being heavy! Could anything be heavier than causing ourselves hurt in the name of losing weight? No matter how big or small the number on the scale was during those years, my spirit weighed a ton. To me, "health" was all about appearance, it had nothing to do with wellness in body, soul, and spirit. Listen to this truth from the *Healthy Is the New Skinny* website: "Health does not have a 'look.' Health has a feeling and the more we can focus on how we feel by caring for ourselves the healthier we will become!" Preach it!

I'm thankful my distorted ways of thinking seem like another lifetime ago. I look back now with concern and compassion for my younger self. What in the world must my poor little mind have been thinking? What messages was I absorbing, to convince me that abusing my sacred, God-crafted body was okay? But the truth is those harmful habits had been deeply tangled into my thoughts and heart for far too long.

How tragic when I could have turned to the Father with an easy yoke and a light burden, to One who was waiting for me to unload all that heaviness onto His strong shoulders. He wants His girls to be whole, to have a lightness and grace of spirit that only He can give them. He wants us to find rest and relief from the constant pressure to look a certain way. Instead of severe restriction God offers unlimited goodness. He surrounds us always with His unfailing love.

Many of you would say "that was/is me too." Have you been there too, in some bathroom, red-eyed and heartsick, wondering how you got to be this messed up, this sick? Seek the help you need from a professional counselor. Know that Jesus is there with you, caring for you, longing to take you into His arms and begin to heal you. He is with you now. His desire for His girls is healing, wholeness, and abundance. The first step is in learning to retrain our minds.

Statistics are valuable in providing a true picture of a topic or issue. In terms of body image, these numbers, from studies cited by the National Eating Disorders Association,[5] blew my mind:

- 35–57 percent of adolescent girls engage in crash dieting, fasting, self-induced vomiting, diet pills, or laxatives. Overweight girls are more likely than healthy-weight girls to engage in such extreme dieting.

  I say: This means over half of God's priceless girls are harming their bodies in order to achieve a particular culturally acceptable "look." Lord, help us!

- Even among girls who are clearly not overweight, over one third report dieting.

  I say: This is so sad. Girls who have a healthy body weight or maybe even an unhealthy thinness are damaging their bodies to attain an impossible standard.

- Four out of five ten-year-olds say that they're afraid of being fat. Forty-two percent of girls in first through third grade wish they were thinner. And, half of girls aged nine or ten claim that they feel better about themselves when they're dieting.

I say: Argh! This one makes me want to wrap my niece in magazine-repellent bubble wrap and never, ever allow a single too-skinny image to cross her path! It makes me want to fill her beautiful little head and heart with all the "you are worthy" messages she can possibly stand to hear.

Fascinatingly, even models often dislike their bodies. There is no such thing as "thin enough"! I will never forget one particular job working for David's Bridal in Chicago. It was a three-day modeling shoot working with five other models. I was the token "curve" model and the other girls were considered straight-size models.

In the world's eyes, these other models were flawless Disney princesses come to life. This client cast each of us to represent a diversified story of beauty, so each model had a different ethnicity, hair color, and look in general. It was beautiful to see the gorgeous diversity in the way God created His girls! But this shoot quickly became strange, confusing, and downright sad. These girls were all between size 0 and 2, and yet they spent the majority of our three days together cruelly picking apart their flaws in an endless loop.

Asian model to Latina model: "If you are trying to cut weight you really shouldn't be eating nuts."

Latina model, looking woefully at the ten almonds in her hand: "I know," she said, making a sad face, "but I'm hungry."

They stood in their undies in front of the mirror, showing each other what they hated about their bodies and what they'd like to change.

"I hate that pooch around my belly," one of them said, pointing to an area of her stomach that could only be described as concave.

"Eeeww," the other would say in agreement. "But my butt is huge compared to yours."

I glanced at both of their butts, so minuscule as to make one wonder how they ever kept their pants up without the aid of belts.

Meanwhile, I stood there, with a real pooch, in no danger of ever losing my pants, wondering what they must be thinking of *me*. It also struck me as *so sad*. Their hatred for their God-given bodies oozed from every perfect pore. What is wrong with us as women that we are never happy with ourselves, regardless of what we look like?

After we had walked the runway many times over three days, wearing the most exquisite dresses you can imagine, the job was done and we parted ways. I enjoyed the work, and the dresses! But oh, how it pained me to hear these dazzling women shame their bodies and each other's food choices.

Other words for "shame"? Dishonor. Debase. Disgrace. Dis-grace. Literally, these "flawless" ladies were dissing grace. It's unbearably distorted, but then again we all do it in one way or another. Ninety percent of us dislike something about our bodies.

Again, it goes back to self-talk. Obviously, these precious women, image bearers of God Almighty, had bought into the lies about where their worth and value lay. How can we bring honor, dignity, and grace into our inner conversations about our body?

After the job wrapped, I went to a local mall and visited a bookstore. I picked up a book all about beauty, how to be beautiful, how to use makeup to your best advantage, etc. Of course, the book's pictures featured photos of the ideal women, the epitome of *beautiful*. You can imagine my shock when one of those picture-perfect faces staring back at me from the glossy pages was the same girl whom I had just witnessed humiliating her body for three days! She had been chosen out of many to typify beauty in this book, yet in real life she personified misery and self-loathing.

Sighing, I shut the slick, shiny book and put it back on the shelf. I ambled over to the food court and ordered a burger. I wasn't "emotionally eating." I wasn't so depressed about how I looked next to the straight-size models that I wanted to drown my sorrows in cheese and meat. No, I ordered a burger because I was hungry, and it was dinnertime. I enjoyed eating it and left with a smile on my face, knowing that whether I subsist on almonds or have an occasional burger for dinner, God loves me just the same!

As a model you sign up to be scrutinized, scolded, and picked apart regardless of what size you are. Whether you are a size 2 or a size 12 you will always be too big or too small according to someone! If you happened to rifle through my purse at any hour night or day, you would find a measuring tape. In this industry, one always has to be ready to take one's measurements. I never know when I will be called on to take stock of my body, giving someone else the chance to say, "Yes, you have the ideal shape and size for this job" or "No, your body is too big/small for this job."

I've worked hard to adjust my thinking during the years I have modeled. To go to a shoot and have a producer say, "Okay, girls, I want all my fatties over here and all my skinnies over there," does *not* promote body positivity. Neither does mealtime at a shoot. Usually clients provide wonderful catered meals for the crew to have on breaks. Obviously, many of the straight-size models are on a strict diet, and by *strict* I mean they barely eat anything. I've lost count of all the times I've sat down for lunch with my sandwich and soup and watched the other girls strip all the meat, cheese, and bread out of their sandwiches and only eat the lettuce, tomatoes, sprouts, etc. In other words, I would eat the actual sandwich and they would eat the plant-based fixings. They nibble on glorified garnish!

I don't know about you, but I believe life is too short to just eat the garnish!

It was these kinds of episodes, along with feeling the heaviness of my body negativity for years, that made me turn the corner early in my modeling career. It was either cave in completely to the world's standard of thinness or change my thought processes. The striving to be skinny had left me exhausted—mentally, physically, emotionally, and spiritually.

I knew this was an impossible endeavor on my own strength. I begged the Lord to change me. I pleaded for understanding to see myself differently. Some days I would pray for strength and realize at the end of the day that He had answered. It felt good to make it through a day where I would eat well and not allow myself to go down that old rabbit hole of worry and anxiety about how that food might make me gain weight.

I prayed that God would help me swap out the constant worry about what others thought of me for a desire to please Him. What did my Father think of me? His love for me and delight in the way He created me became my focus. I learned to say, "Who cares?" when I thought someone might be judging my size.

I realized that striving to look like someone else was a form of idolatry. I was driving myself crazy trying to change myself, running after an image of someone else. When we look at another person's appearance and wish we had exactly what they have, it defeats God's purpose in making us one of a kind. We must stop running after what God *hasn't* intended for us and start finding joy in what He *has* given us. We also need to confess and repent.

"Repent" might sound a little harsh but I think this step is a healthy one. It simply means humbling ourselves before the Lord, our Father, our Maker: *I'm sorry for mistreating myself and abusing what You have created on purpose, Lord. I am Your special creation and I am sorry for not treating myself the way You intended. Help me honor and value the body You have given me. Help me be healthy, body and soul.* This humble prayer allows us to leave the guilt and shame at His feet and walk with Him in new freedom.

Finally, I began to get serious about my self-talk in regard to my body. I realized that the things I was saying to myself were nasty things I would never in a million years say to a friend, a sister, or—horrors!—a niece or daughter.

Whereas I used to look in the mirror, sigh dramatically, and think:

- *I wish these clothes looked different on my body.*
- *I hate the way I look.*

- *Gross—you are gross!*
- Plus many more destructive things.

Now those days are gone. But the change didn't happen overnight.

Where are you at in this process? You may be thinking of some of the fat-shaming things you have said to yourself, maybe even today.

Part of the problem is we condone this mean self-talk, don't we? We excuse and tolerate this cruelty in ourselves *to* ourselves! And our Father who formed us with such tender care says, "Dearest one, don't talk that way to My beloved girl!"

We need to take a strong stand against this kind of inner messaging. Next time you're making an *ewww* face at yourself in the mirror, and you sense those shaming, vicious thoughts bubbling up from that inner cauldron, just stop. Stop!

"Nope, not gonna allow it! I will not tolerate anyone saying mean-spirited things about my body, especially me!"

Now, this doesn't mean you will be living in a delusional wad of bubblegum: "Hey, girl—those thighs are ready for the cover of the swimsuit edition!"

The point is to accept reality, but reshape your body image from the inside out. To learn to be kind and compassionate to this amazing, singular frame God has given you. To appreciate all that your body can do, instead of looking at the things you can't do.

Instead of offering harsh critiques to our mirror images, we must learn to offer praise and thanks to God for His great gifts.

"Thanks, Father, for a healthy body, a strong heart-beat, and for my blue eyes/long eyelashes/shapely kneecaps/pretty skin, etc."

What can you thank God for right now?

The wonderful truth is that we have control over our thoughts! One of the biggest revelations of my life was realizing I could think the things I wanted to think. I could get rid of the thoughts I didn't want to think! I learned to prepare my mind before entering a situation, anticipating what feelings were bound to pop up. If I was going to a casting, say, where a hundred girls were higher on the *beauty scale* according to the world, I would go in mentally prepared to fight the nasty thoughts.

There is no such thing as a beauty scale, *and besides, all of God's girls are 10s! In Christ, I am worthy, valuable, lovable, and holy.*

Practicing this over and over made it natural for me to go there in my mind without much effort at all.

God has given His girls a way to overcome damaging thoughts and behaviors, and gain the self-control we need to kick body negativity to the curb! It's a matter of taking charge of your life—His way. Second Corinthians 10:5 tells us that we are to "take captive every thought to make it obedient to Christ."

Captive—caged, imprisoned, incarcerated. Yes, that's exactly where our body trash talk should go: to prison! Once we get in the habit of tossing those trashy thoughts, we can throw away the key and live our lives with new and exhilarating freedom. Confront your harmful thoughts:

No way, Jose! This—this obsession with/revulsion for my muffin top—is not happening.

Turn them over to God and become who He sees you can be. It requires some intentional work to take your thoughts captive each time they pop into your mind. But it is possible with the help of the Holy Spirit.

Gradually, thought-swap by thought-swap, prayer by prayer, confession by confession, I built up a sort of immunity to the incredible body negativity I had nurtured for so long. And with the immunity came something new and shocking—a care, compassion, and even celebration for the body God had given me. Instead of clawing apart the flaws I saw in the mirror and allowing myself to wallow in self-hatred—let's call it what it is—I learned to give proper thanks to God who fashioned me to be beautiful and singular. He made you to be beautiful and singular too! Do you believe it?

When our minds shift, our hearts swing with freedom and joy. We start to get it—that health, beauty, and wellness come in many shapes and sizes, and that being healthy is a feeling, not an impossible way to look. We discover that every shape and size and weight is worthy of respect, love, and acceptance, including our own. Our sails are filled up with the God-breathed desire to be the best and healthiest edition of ourselves.

Like the little brown-haired girl with the ponytail and scone crumbs on her tummy, we have our Father's rapt attention, His total engagement. No matter if we are a size 2, 12, or 22, He smiles at us encouragingly, leaning in on His elbows to listen closer to our every utterance.

Everything you say is so important to Him. His eyes do not leave yours, and He is enthralled to be there with you now, spending time with His daughter. He has no desire to be anywhere else but by your side.

You are beautiful! When the world says, "You're not skinny enough," God says something else: "You are my treasure. I crafted you with fathomless love. Come to Me with your heaviness of spirit and let Me carry it. Follow Me as I show you a path of fullness, lightness, freedom, and plenty."

Beauty Box

1. What were you taught about your body and looks as a child? Were you encouraged to respect and care for your body, or treat it carelessly to achieve a certain look?

2. Write down a list of ten things that you like about yourself—be sure they are things not related to weight or physical appearance—then get feedback from five people close to you on which things they like about you. It will lift you up!

3. On a scale of 1 to 10, how much prominence does your body get in the big picture of your life? Many of us can relate to blogger Hallie Graves, who realized with a shock that she was giving her body an 11. Do you give your body an inflated, distorted importance? Take it down to a 5, or whatever number seems to represent balance to you. For Hallie, she tended to go to both extremes, either neglecting the body God had given her and doing nothing to care for it or being obsessed with it, crowding out the pursuit of her best spiritual and emotional self. Join her in this prayer and start giving fitting and right value to each area of your life: "Lord, I don't want this to be an 11. I want you to be my only 11. Please teach me how to devalue this."[6]

4. Do you feel as if your size determines your future, a good outcome or bad outcome, or even your happiness?

5. Studies show we are exposed to 10.4 hours of media each day. Magazine covers in the grocery

store, TV ads, and social media posts all stress the importance of a woman's appearance above all else. "As a result," says the website *Healthy Is the New Skinny*, "our mind, bodies, and spirits have suffered dramatically." Be intentionally watchful about those messages. If a magazine picture makes you feel bad about yourself, toss it. Log off and take a walk when you feel those messages are becoming too powerful.

6. Next time you are tempted to indulge in self-shaming, imagine yourself saying the exact same thing to a pal. Apply the "Would you say it to a friend?" rule as a test for your self-talk.

5
BEAUTIFUL

I always knew I wanted to go to beauty school. My parents were ever supportive, but other people gave me pushback. After all, beauty school is not exactly a path to prestige and fortune.

"Oh, don't do *that*," people would say, "You don't want to do that—you won't make any money!"

The subtext being the only way to flourish in this world is to get a job that will make you lots of money. Because we all know that money *can* buy you love, right? Sigh.

My senior year of high school I led a Bible study for freshman girls, which sparked a desire in me to encourage and guide young girls. I wondered briefly if I should go to Bible college and pursue a degree in women's ministry.

But the tug toward beauty school was undeniable and, I can now see, God-orchestrated. I signed up for the yearlong course and felt peace.

God can still use me in beauty school, I thought. And He did. For me, beauty school—ironically enough—was a key part of my figuring out the role of outer and inner beauty in my life and in the lives of those God had set on my path.

On my first day of school it felt as though the heavens had opened up and all my prayers were going to be answered. If you've ever wondered what beauty school was like, you've come to the right place.

Beauty school novices are started out in the "Junior Room," which is to say, far from the heads of anyone with a pulse. You begin your training on mannequin heads, a step I fully endorse. Later on in beauty school, when we were working on each other's heads, I'll never forget the day when one of my fellow junior beauticians accidentally cut off all my hair. I looked as though a blind monkey had been turned loose on my head!

My creative juices got a workout, and I devoted all day, every day to all things beauty. We learned about the muscles of the body so we could give our future clients neck massages. We practiced doing nails by giving each other manicures. Even the somewhat grinding challenge of completing ninety perms was fun. Sure, doing a hot iron set on Madge the Mannequin wasn't the most fun, but later, when the newbies were unleashed into "the salon," I thoroughly enjoyed getting to know the little old ladies who would come in for their "roller sets." Their kindness, wisdom, humor, and stories enriched my life and reminded me that it's not only the young and glamorous who are beautiful. I was beginning to understand that there are different kinds of beauty

I was elected president of my beauty school, and for the first time in my life, I felt like I was using my creative abilities for a purpose. I received a vicarious thrill from making my clients and friends look as beautiful as possible. In fact, I had a fierce desire to help others feel and look their best, partly because I hated not feeling good enough myself and wanted to help others avoid that hurt. At the same time, I still considered pursuing women's ministry as a way to answer my questions about Christian women and self-worth. Later I would see that God had already placed me in a women's ministry—the beauty industry.

Do you think you're beautiful? You are—there's no doubt in my mind. But we'll talk about that in a minute. For now, let's figure out what being beautiful really means.

I was surprised to find out that *pretty* and *beautiful* mean very different things.

> **Pretty:** attractive in a delicate way without being truly beautiful or handsome. Example: "a pretty little girl with an engaging grin."[7]
> **Beautiful:** having beauty; possessing qualities that give great pleasure or satisfaction to see, hear, think about, etc.; delighting the senses or mind. Example: "Located on one of the most beautiful and untouched coastlines in America, this recreational area has much to offer."[8]

This is why the book you are holding in your hands is not called *You Are Pretty*. Yes, we talked about the pursuit of prettiness in chapter 3, and about being a "pretty-does" kind of girl, but *pretty* pales in comparison to *beautiful*.

So many things can be beautiful without having a thing to do with small pores or sculpted abs. A sunset is beautiful—so is a baby's newborn skin. City lights twinkling at night. Stars twinkling at night! Fireworks.

The Sistine Chapel. A beloved pet's silky ears. An eagle soaring in the sky.

My mom is beautiful—a woman who sees the best in absolutely everyone. Mom relentlessly seeks out the good and positive and praiseworthy in every person she encounters, even those most of us see as damaged and ugly. To me, this quality of hers shines bright, because the most beautiful people in the world are those who see the beauty in others, even when it's hidden.

In this way, she's like her Father, my Father, and yours. He sees the "inner self," as Peter puts it in 1 Peter 3:4. The hidden person of your heart is precious to God, as is the "unfading charm" of someone who is compassionate and at peace with themselves and those around them. That's beautiful.

Let's challenge ourselves to crack open our faulty, narrow definition of beauty to find a pearl of truth that will change our lives. Let's reject the idea that beauty is all about plump lips, chiseled cheekbones, and flat tummies. Let's learn to embrace God's definition of beauty. We will never be the same!

But first, let me tell you a story of a girl who was deemed beautiful in the eyes of the world, but her "hidden person of the heart" was anything but (1 Pet. 3:4 ESV).

I couldn't believe what came out of that gorgeous woman's mouth.

This fellow model—let's call her Amber—was known for being difficult to work with from the perspective of her colleagues, including me. She swore like a sailor, even calling her mom a dumb b—— in my presence. Amber radiated unhappiness like a small-scale radioactive leak. She complained constantly about her mother, her NBA boyfriend, her body, and everyone around her. Snippy, snappy, grouchy, sulky—we all gave her a wide berth whenever she was around.

One time we were on a shoot together for a home-shopping channel. How this works is that each model gets a rack of clothing that they have to change in and out of lickety split. It's a blur of activity and a flurry of garments as everyone tries to hop in and out of their outfits.

Somehow, Amber's pieces got hung on my rack, resulting in the dresser putting me in her clothes. Which actually is no big deal to most people and happens all the time in this hectic environment.

I made the grave mistake of walking by Amber in "her" fur coat and thigh-high boots, oblivious to the switcheroo.

I felt her stunning green eyes on me before she spat to her friend: "I guess some girls think it's okay to steal other people's clothing."

"What? Oh, I am sorry!" I said. "I honestly didn't know these were yours! They were on my rack and so I just didn't know." There was no time to change clothing at that point.

Arms crossed and lips pinched, Amber did not relax her stance in the slightest.

What she was really mad about was that now she would not be able to wear the glamorous getup, which would have shown her off to her best advantage. She would have to put on flannel pajamas or something that would put her in a less fantastic light. I understood where she was coming from and regretted the incident! Trust me, a few minutes in fabulous boots were not worth Amber's wrath. But despite my annoyance with her, I also felt compassion. Her "hidden person of the heart" was screaming for love, acceptance, and kindness, and it wasn't pretty—not at all.

As I've worked in the beauty industry, both in modeling and hair and makeup, one thing has become obvious to me: Everyone focuses on their unattractive traits and ignores their attractive traits. If this were a pie chart, the emphasis on the negative would represent about a 90 percent slice of the whole. Girls with curvy bodies want less curvy bodies. Thin girls with flat bodies want fluffier bodies. Curly-haired girls want straight hair and straight-haired girls want curls. It's a cycle of chronic discontentment.

When I do hair and makeup for weddings, I get to hear people talk about their insecurities on full blast.

"I want to cover my big ears."

"I hate my nose."

"I have to hide these wrinkles."

I always try to listen to what they are telling me. These women are bridesmaids, brides, mothers-of-the-bride and -groom, and when they sit down in my chair they are often concerned about their perceived flaws. They are almost always nervous that they will not feel beautiful on a big day that means everything to them.

I challenge myself to do whatever it is that I can to make them leave with a smile on their face. I want them to know they are beautiful in spite of their round faces and prominent noses or whatever it is they are consumed with. Immediately, I start to focus on the good.

"Wow, you have the most beautiful brown eyes! Let's style your hair to show those beauties off!"

"Your skin is really pretty. This updo will highlight your great cheekbones."

"That smile of yours could melt a heart of stone! I have just the lip color to show it off even more."

By the time my clients leave my chair I will have raved about their eyes, focused on their sweet spirit, and reminded them of their positive qualities. Suddenly, there is a key shift in thinking, and being beautiful for their special occasion is not only possible but realized. In return, I feel myself shining from the inside out—it's a win-win.

We all have the power to help others shine. Studies show that when we compliment someone, their energy rises 40 percent! And we get a boost too, when we make others feel good.

Think about it. When you hear (or say) the phrase, "She is beautiful," is it about someone's appearance or an inner quality? We are entrenched in a culture that teaches us one definition of beautiful and one definition alone: good looks.

God measures beauty so differently! He gives us clues throughout Scripture as to what defines a beautiful woman—or man.

I am intrigued by the story of how David was chosen as king over Israel. I always had the impression that David was an exceptionally handsome man, haven't you? I mean, all of those wives! And he just seemed to smolder with passion, whether he was talking about someone he loved or God Himself.

But apparently, David's brothers were *extraordinarily* good-looking!

When Samuel was deciding who would be the king

of Israel, he had all of Jesse's sons pass before him, and time after time, Samuel thought that surely one of these young men would be the next king. I can see it all play out:

Brother #1 walks the gauntlet of *Project Kingway* or whatever path Samuel had these guys walk by him on. He looks like a swarthy Chris Pine—striking and manly. And Samuel thinks for sure this is the guy. But no. God said, "Next."

Brother #2 strolls on by, and he looks like Dwayne "The Rock" Johnson. Tall. Fit! Able to fling a spear and fly over a rock outcropping at the same time! If Israel had a *People* magazine, he would have been named "The Sexiest Man Alive."

And then two more saunter in, and they are clones of the Hemsworth brothers, except with dark eyes and hair. By this time, Samuel is agog. "You've got to be kidding me, right, Lord? These are very kingly specimens of humanity here!"

It's at this point that God breaks in with a word for the ages: First Samuel 16:7 says, "But the LORD said to Samuel, 'Do not look on his appearance or on the height of his stature, because I have rejected him. For the LORD sees not as man sees: man looks on the outward appearance, but the LORD looks on the heart'" (ESV).

I love the Message version too: "Looks aren't everything. Don't be impressed with his looks and stature. I've already eliminated him. GOD judges persons differently than humans do. Men and women look at the face; GOD looks into the heart."

In other words, all of Jesse's sons were tall and muscly and easy on the eyes, but God wasn't interested in any of that. He was interested in what Samuel couldn't see but He could: Someone with a heart after His own, someone like the shorter, less physically impressive kid brother. Someone like David.

God was saying to Samuel, "Hey, if you stand two guys next to each other and one is The Rock who's adored for his good looks and muscle and the other guy is more average-looking but loves Me more than anything, *he* is the one I choose. His hidden person of the heart burns with passion to know Me and serve Me, and that is precious."

And He says to us the same thing: "Dearest, if you with your size 16 jeans and your acne scars and double chin stand next to a model like Amber, I see that her beauty is sadly limited to physical beauty. I see that you love Me with your whole heart and in My eyes you are far more beautiful than she is."

God looks at our hearts because the most important features of a person are never what we see but the things we don't see. And what we cannot see, God can.

You are God's masterpiece, His perfect work of art, created to do "good things" planned for you before the dawn of time! And because you bear His image— you take after your Father—you carry His creative spirit within you.

Listen to what writer Mary DeMuth says on the website *Christianity Today*:

> I rejoice in what I create. It's an inbred trait, imparted when God breathed life into us. He is creative—and his children are too. We enjoy showing off what we've made.
>
> So is it any surprise that God is proud of his creation—us?...You are God's child, dearly

loved, fully settled in your worth. Just as parents are proud of their children, God is proud of you.[9]

In our most insecure moments, when we feel empty, lonely, and disempowered, we can fill up with the truth—that we are dearly loved, God's work of art sent for an artless world.

Time for another thought-swap: Let's pay attention to truth instead of lies. Let's concentrate on God's values instead of our culture's unrealities.

Let's remind ourselves, daily, hourly, that being beautiful is not defined by a pre-manufactured clothing size, sculpted thighs, a supermodel butt, pouty lips, or clear, wrinkle-free skin. Can we lay down our idols at the foot of the cross? Can we do a 180 and walk straight into the arms of steadfast Love, waiting for us all this time?

According to the Dove Foundation, only 2 percent of women would describe themselves as beautiful.[10] Are you in that 2 percent? Do you know anyone in that 2 percent?

We must work hard to redefine "beautiful." Only then can we absorb a life-giving definition. Despite the huge number of women who believe they are not beautiful, the majority surveyed believe the following about *other* women:

- Seventy-seven percent strongly agree that beauty can be attained through personality, spirit, and other qualities that have nothing to do with looks.
- Sixty-six percent—two thirds—strongly agree that physical attractiveness is about how one

looks, while being beautiful is much more of who a person is. Women grade confidence, joy, goodness, and humor as powerful elements of being beautiful, along with the more traditional attributes of physical appearance, body weight and shape, and even a sense of style.

Who do you think of when the term *inner beauty* comes up? I think of my mom, and I also think of Sharisse, one of the producers of *Coupled,* whom I worked with when I was a cast member on the show.

Sharisse is not just smart, she's wise. She's adventurous, but with a calmness and peace I so admire. Sometimes the craziness on set was too much for any human to handle. Meanwhile, Sharisse would be in the background, working hard, radiating strength, wisdom, and a much-needed composure drawn from a well of peace.

Who are the inner beauty queens in our lives, those bright souls who often get overlooked by a world obsessed with appearance? A few of my friends weighed in with their thoughts:

From Brenda: My mother-in-law. She makes you feel known and loved.

From Noreen: My mom, whose name was Nellie, which means shining light. She was a shining light to all who knew her. She especially taught her children to be kind.

From Jamie: My friend Rebecca. A music teacher by training, she started doing triathlons when her three adopted children were younger as an outlet for processing their RAD (reactive attachment disorder). Even though her children could not show her love in return, she poured her heart and soul into raising them. She is my hero.

From Cass: Susan, because she first introduced me to Jesus and showed me how to really love a husband.

From Jodi: Mom. I watched her care for my dad during his seven years of cancer—making him her ministry. As he was dying, she faced the unknown with grace and tackled tasks that were way out of her comfort zone. And now I watch her adjust to her new normal, still leaning into God for strength. She is an example of true beauty.

From Traci: A lady in our church named Janet. She lives with contentment, is fiercely loyal to her church, prays for her family, and still serves with a willing heart.

From Susan: Rachel. She has an endless energy for the things of God. She is selfless. She has an inner knowing that keeps her going in the darkest days. She trusts God for every outcome and waits on Him on her knees.

From Lori: Right before my precious aunt Gladys died at age fifty-three, I sat by her bedside and looked at my once pretty aunt, emaciated, shrunken, her once peaches-and-cream skin tones now sallow and gray. At one point, she asked me how she could pray for me, and it made me realize how caring, courageous, and strong Aunt Gladys was. I have missed her all these years but I carry with me the image of her in that bed, broken and beautiful.

Sniff! I am a little overcome as I think about these magnificent women and their inner splendor, shining among us like stars in the sky (see Philippians 2:15).

From these vignettes, we see that inner beauty means different things to different people. Some women are beautiful for their ability to make others feel known and loved and cared for. Others are praised for their wisdom, trust in God, contentment, and dignity in their darkest hours.

What can we learn from these women? How can we increase our beauty quotient?

An inner kind of radiance can be nurtured. Here are some behaviors that belong in the mix. Live out these, and glow with beauty in all the right ways, both to yourself and others.

HUMOR

Laughter makes everything go down easier, even in truly sad situations. Someone who makes you laugh is someone you want to be with, and of course you feel great when you make someone else laugh. The Proverbs 31 woman "can laugh at the days to come."

Don't worry if you're not Tina Fey or Kate McKinnon—your sense of humor is as matchless as your DNA, and yours rejuvenates everyone you meet. The Bible says, "A cheerful heart is good medicine" (Prov. 17:22 NIV). Humor is a healing agent for yourself and those around you. What could be more beautiful than a funny girl?

COMPASSION

Compassion is empathy, kindness, and a willingness to help alleviate the suffering of others. It's listening patiently and well to someone who needs to talk, and thinking of ways to make a fellow traveler's path a little easier. Jesus has always shown unlimited capacity for compassion. He showed us the way through His concern for the crippled man at the pool of Bethesda; the woman taken in adultery; the woman at Jacob's well; the daughter of Jairus; Lazarus, brother of Mary and Martha. Each needed help and He gave it to them. Compassion is a healing agent for yourself and those around you. What could be more beautiful than a compassionate girl?

WISDOM

Believe it or not, you can be wise at any age. "According to the data, between ages twenty-five to seventy-five, the correlation between age and wisdom is zero," says Adam Grant in *Psychology Today*. "Wisdom emerges not from experience itself, but rather from reflecting thoughtfully on the lessons gained from experience."[11] Wisdom tries to understand, not judge; it considers many viewpoints and all the colors of the rainbow, not just black and white. Pray for wisdom to the God who gives generously and without reproach! Our Father loves to answer our prayers for insight. Wisdom is a healing agent for yourself and those around you. What could be more beautiful than a wise girl?

WORSHIP

Yes, worship helps us shine with a divine kind of beautiful. Worship renews our minds and reminds us of God's worth and beauty, which takes our minds off our own beauty idols. I find so much comfort from worship! So often I will be riding in my car during a busy day and a defeating thought pops into my head. Just like that, my mood sags and I feel down in the dumps.

I may have left a meeting where I did a poor job at communicating and feel like a total idiot. Or I may be having an "ugly day," complete with frizzy hair, bloating, and that terrible feeling you have when a monster zit is about to bust through the surface of your chin. And the downward spiral has begun, my mood sliding down that slippery slope of self-loathing. At this point, Satan is right on board with his minions, heckling me about all the ways in which I lack and am therefore unlovable.

I choose to combat that by worshipping audibly, whenever I can (silently works too!):

God, You are so good to me! I know You created me with purpose to do big things for Your glory! I know You tell me I am fearfully and wonderfully made! God, thank You for loving me and creating me special and unique!

Friend, try this, and say it like you mean it! The saying "worship recalibrates the heart" has proven to be true in my life. It's the cure for self-absorption and the ultimate idol buster.

"Worship is the arena in which God recalibrates our hearts, reforms our desires, and rehabituates our loves," says James K. A. Smith in his book *You Are What You Love: The Spiritual Power of Habit*.[12] "Worship isn't just something we do; it is where God does something to us. Worship is the heart of discipleship because it is the gymnasium in which God retrains our hearts."

Yes, through worship, God fine-tunes us. He brings our messy thoughts into line and upgrades our desires, from wanting this world's version of beauty to wanting *His* beauty.

Sis, try this, please! Giving God glory for making you does nothing less than transforms you. Thanking God for His goodness in creating you, even if there are things you want to work on, has so much power. Worship is a healing agent for yourself and those around you. What could be more beautiful than a worshipful girl?

Humor, compassion, wisdom, and a spirit of worship—let's cultivate these beautiful qualities in ourselves, and watch for them in others. After all, the most beautiful person is she who sees the beauty in others.

There are many ways to make the world a more beautiful place. Maybe you'll go to beauty school, like I did, and learn to bring out the loveliness in others. Using your gifts and abilities is a way to honor your Creator!

Beauty matters, but we all need to nurture our "hidden person of the heart," knowing that this is precious to our Father (1 Pet. 3:4 ESV).

If we are to believe we are more than the sum of our parts, more than just buns of steel and glossy hair and delicate cheekbones—or jiggly buns, frizzy hair, and a double chin—we have to make heart space. We must dethrone the pursuit of the world's *beautiful* to make space for the things that will matter one thousand years from now: Knowing Jesus better, serving others, loving people well, and even just doing what He's called us to do in the day-to-day.

Seek forgiveness for the ways you've pursued a false salvation through striving for our culture's standard of beauty. Ask Him to help you make peace with the way God made you. You will find deliverance and relief. You will escape the relentless struggle to be someone you are not and were never meant to be. You are rescued by the One who made you beautiful.

Physical beauty will fade over time, but spiritual beauty is timeless.

Beauty Box

1. Is it difficult to think of yourself as God's masterpiece? Express your thoughts and feelings to God. Pray, *Help me to settle into my worth.*

2. "According to the Dove Foundation, only 2 percent of women would describe themselves as beautiful." Are you in that 2 percent? Do you know anyone in that 2 percent?

3. Who do you think of when the term *inner beauty* comes up?

4. Do you have an "Amber" in your life? Pray that God would show you her hurting heart through His eyes.

5. Focus on the good things God has given you, and you will notice your attention begin to shift. Listen, we *all* have things we won't feel completely happy with. It's easy to look at our problem areas with a laser beam, but when we look at the big picture—health, a great smile, a kind, giving heart, *and* a fabulous new haircut, you'll find that joy in God's creation!

6. Say "awe" at other forms of beauty. "Awe" is a dramatic feeling with the power to inspire, heal, change our thinking, and bring people together. Feeling wonder at God's beauty takes our mind off our obsession with our own perceived lack of it. A starry night. An ocean or huge lake, with waves rolling in. Someone's incredible voice as she sings a song you love. A masterpiece in an art museum, or even a stunning turn of phrase in your favorite book.[13]

7. Let's stop comparing ourselves to one another. Next time you start to compare, stop yourself and look for something beautiful in the other person and in yourself. It's way more fun to appreciate each other than to tear each other down.

8. Tuck these verses away. You'll need them every day!

   - "She opens her mouth with wisdom, and the teaching of kindness is on her tongue." (Prov. 31:26 ESV)
   - "God is within her, she will not fall." (Ps. 46:5)
   - "She is clothed with strength and dignity, and she laughs without fear of the future." (Prov. 31:25 NLT)

6
ELITE

"Hello, this is Kasia from Elite. We think you are beautiful and would like to have you come in for a meeting."

Wait—what? I had to pick up my eighteen-year-old jaw from the ground about fifteen times before my brain processed the words. Me, Ashley, the one who had felt overlooked and insufficient all her life, had been chosen by Elite, the prestigious modeling agency that represented the models from my absolute favorite show, *America's Next Top Model*!

When I listened to the voicemail it felt like the greatest, most fulfilling moment of my existence. Completely and utterly surreal. For the first time, I was being pursued because I was special and different from others. To be acknowledged as a "stand out" from the crowd, just for being me, was something I deeply craved.

That million-bucks feeling? It makes the world go round. People run after that feeling hard; they'll do anything to grab hold of it. It's probably one of the top five most-craved human desires in history. Pursued for your singular purpose, your "elite" reason for being!

If you're an actress you might dream about winning an Oscar, because it would mean that your passion is recognized by others, your work is exceptional. At work, you may long to be at the top of the company or to be recognized for a special accomplishment on a project. At school you may want to get not only an A but glowing feedback from a teacher you admire. These goals drive us to get what we want.

Maybe, like Julia Roberts in *Notting Hill*, you're just a girl, standing in front of a boy, asking him to love her. When we fancy someone like Julia fancied Hugh Grant, and he tells us how special we are to him, it means the sun, moon, and stars! We live to be someone's exclusive choice, don't we?

Yes, we thirst for attention, but I believe it goes much deeper than that. We know in our innermost being that we want to mean something. We want to be someone's best, to be selected as the top option. And we try and try and try to have that feeling validated, no matter what the cost.

For me, at age eighteen, receiving the call from Elite was that glittering moment. *This is going to be the answer to all my problems*, I assured myself. *This will finally solve the question of my worthiness. Now I have a real reason to feel complete*. Except, of course, that I didn't.

Where does your purpose in life come from? Your affirmation? Have you ever felt like you would finally feel whole and content, if only this relationship or that circumstance or a certain prized accomplishment would swing your way? If your skin cleared up and you finally lost that last ten pounds?

For years, I pinned my sense of worth on whether or not I would cut my weight, that boy would finally crush on me, or that dream would come true at long last. But I learned something the hard way. If you can't find meaning, value, and approval from within—the person made and loved by God—it's going to be even harder to find if we are depending on someone else to provide it.

I have a question for you: What or who do you depend on for your sense of meaning?

- A guy?
- A grade in school?
- A part in the play?
- A sought-after achievement?

Then ask yourself, *Was it worth it? Did I find my life's purpose when my heart finally hit its target?*

Oh, high school. What a blessing! Okay, now I am being snarky. At the time, it sure felt like more of a mild curse, a chronic feeling of discontent, not quite fitting in, and loneliness.

After my family moved when I was in ninth grade, I went through so many phases. The first phase was, oddly enough, acceptance. As a newcomer, I had that new girl glow. I was an unknown quantity, and therefore fresh blood, a short-lived novelty.

I was accepted into most any circle, including the rich, popular kids, the slightly rebellious crowd, the good kids who were involved in all the clubs, and the sporty clique. The only problem was, I just couldn't find one that fit me. I was friends with everyone and yet not close friends with anyone. Have you ever felt that way?

By my junior year I had come to the conclusion that this sort of neither in nor out status was okay—not great, but tolerable. What other choice did I have? My heart of hearts hungered for a kindred spirit, but at least no one was sliding banana peels in my path or shoving my face into the cafeteria Jell-O.

I did my thing by going to school, hanging with whoever was there at the moment and trying to be a good quasi-friend. My chief joy was my job as a barista at a tropical-themed coffee shop called Cup O' Cabana. The ole Cabana still ranks as one of my very favorite jobs of all time. We had the world's best cookies, and my favorite thing in all of Fooddom is a chocolate chip cookie.

I knew that at my school I belonged everywhere and nowhere, which is an empty feeling. But if I could just make it through high school, eke whatever I could out of it, and graduate, *then* I would go on to find happiness and fulfillment. Have you ever thought that, if a situation or circumstance in your life changed, then you would finally be fulfilled?

I had no sense of the profound purpose I could have had, if I had placed my need for affirmation into the right hands.

I had no idea I was living my life as a chicken, when I could have been soaring through school as an eagle. (I promise, comparing myself to a chicken will make sense in a bit.)

So it came as a gigantic shock when, one day in senior year, I heard my name called over the intercom. "Your 2007 Adrian High School homecoming court will consist of the following students *you* voted in: Stephanie, Jillian, Kayla, Nicole, Brooke…" I tuned it out, so sure was I of having no involvement in this announcement whatsoever.

"And finally…Ashley."

WHAT?! I was thunderstruck. I can't believe I didn't fall out of my desk right then and there in government class.

Stephanie, Jillian, Kayla, Nicole, Brooke—*them* I could understand being nominated. They had been at the school since kindergarten, were heavily involved in all the important things that would normally land a girl on the homecoming court.

The only reason I could think of for my inclusion was because I genuinely talked to everyone from all grades. That's it. There must have been enough warm bodies who knew I existed to squeeze me through, but surely that wasn't enough to win homecoming court status. Apparently it was.

I didn't care! I just knew it meant an opportunity to hit the tanning bed, buy a pretty dress, and get my nails done! For once, I felt affirmed. I meant something to these people, whoever they were, who cast their ballots for me.

Homecoming night arrived and I took my umber self for a stroll on the football field in front of the student body. I was 100 percent sure that I wouldn't win; I was just there to enjoy the ride. I had it on good authority that the votes had been counted and Kayla had won, which made perfect sense. She was on student council; had tons of friends, glossy blonde hair, and blue eyes; and weighed about 110 soaking wet. Thin, pretty, popular—the whole package.

We had been told that this year, a ring would be given to the queen, not a crown. A simple band from the nicest jewelry store in our small town—a charming little keepsake for the winner. My source told me that the ring had been fitted by student council members for the girl who supposedly was to win (another Kayla confirmation). I stood there on the little bleacher stands, smiling what I thought was a pageant smile. My dearest hope at that point was being named second runner-up—but no, the second and then the first runners-up were called and neither of them was me. Deflated, I zoned out, gearing up to paste that sash-worthy beam on my face and embrace the winner. That's about the time there was a seismic shift in the universe.

"And the homecoming queen of 2007 is…Ashley Reitz!!!"

It made the earth. Move. Under my feet. You know, just like the song. I gasped loudly and clamped my hand over my mouth. You could have knocked me over with a feather. Good thing the homecoming king came right then and guided me along in my state of walking catatonia.

It was a mountaintop moment, to be sure, yet already the perfection of it began to tarnish. Part of me instantly felt undeserving, and another part was scared, because I knew already there would be some jealous backlash. The ring fit perfectly.

I'll never forget leaving the school that night to go home. I did not attend any after-parties. First of all, parties were not my thing. I didn't have any close friends to drag me along. All I wanted to do was go home and spend time with my family.

As I walked into the parking lot I saw a few other girls from the homecoming court huddled together. They were whispering away. When they saw me coming they quickly hushed up, and collectively flashed a fake smile at me.

Just like that, I was down in the valley again, insecure and vulnerable. I've never had a moment of such happiness go *poof* so quickly. Even though I had "won" the supposed admiration of enough people to be crowned homecoming queen, the victory was hollow. From the time of the court announcement over the loudspeaker, I had placed all my "eggs," all my personal sense of meaning, value, and approval, in one basket, in the hands of my classmates. Clarity like cold water splashed me in the face. I had actually attained the height of validation for my worth—or at least the height at Adrian High School. I even had a ring to prove it! Yet I was no more significant or even loved than before, when I was just a nice girl in math class who remembered people's names. Even though I had been chosen as the "stand out" girl—a dream come true!—absolutely nothing had changed.

I wish I had known then what I know now: Our worth cannot be validated by a human being or the accolades of this earth. It's like that stamp of approval we beg for is made of disappearing ink.

Worthy
Valued
Exceptional
The Best

When we see those words in relation to ourselves, we get a little high, don't we? We feel like a million bucks, for a while. Our inner price tag seems to go up, up, up. We suddenly know why it is we get up in the morning, because our raison d'être—the very justification for our existence—has been confirmed. Unfortunately, that sought-after achievement, guy, or status delivers a short-lived satisfaction. That longed-for stamp of approval fades into oblivion.

That night in 2007, I knew the truth in the school parking lot when those girls turned on me. My surprise victory didn't confer long-term worth, value, or peace to me. I was back to struggling with insecurity and the sense of not belonging.

What is your reason for being right now? Your end game? Whether it be a love note from the man of your dreams, an award for excellence, a crown on your head, or a post that goes viral... none of it lasts.

After a high like that, life moves on for us and those around us. The things we think have defined us change or maybe even go away altogether.

I know this now: When we try to gain prestige in this world's eyes, even if we succeed, we end up feeling empty. But living into God's purposes for us makes us exclusive and influential in His kingdom.

Another question for you: Are you a chicken or an eagle?

I'm being serious right now. If we are ever going to live out God's elite purposes for our lives, we first have to figure out *who we think we are*. Because our beliefs about ourselves—about our worth, what we are capable of—can hold us back. If you believe, for example, that your life's meaning is found in a number on the scale, or a particular guy's attention, or entrance into the social group of your dreams, you have a low view of your purpose and potential. (You know by now I had a terribly low view of my own purpose for years.) If you believe you are a chicken, you behave accordingly.

Many of us were brought up with a limited understanding of our potential. I was. I thought my goal in life was to be skinnier, prettier, more *something* in order to feel accepted and lovable. This pursuit left me empty and exhausted, pining for significance.

Our beliefs can also propel us forward into our purpose, designed before the sun and moon were placed in the sky! This is eagle living, and it's a true high.

A friend once told me the story below and it clicked with me that we too often settle and live beneath what God has created us for. It's time to ask yourself, "What do I believe about myself?"

"A man found an eagle's egg and put it in the nest of a barnyard hen. The eagle hatched with a brood of chicks and grew up with them. All his life the eagle did what the barnyard chicks did, thinking he was a barnyard chick. He scratched the earth for worms and insects, he clucked and cackled. And he would thrash his wings and fly a few feet in the air. Years passed and the eagle grew very old. One day he saw a magnificent bird above him in the cloudless sky. It glided in graceful majesty among the powerful wind currents, with scarcely a beat of its strong golden wings. The eagle looked up in awe. 'Who's that?' he asked.

" 'That's the eagle, the king of the birds,' said his neighbor. 'He belongs to the sky. We belong to the earth—we are chickens.' So the eagle lived and died a chicken, for that's what he thought he was."[14]

Do you belong to the earth or to the sky? Do you believe you were designed to scratch for grubs in the dirt or take your rightful place at your Father's banqueting table? Are there any ways that you see yourself as a barnyard chicken and are not aware of your potential grandeur? You could soar like an eagle. What would that look like for you? But first you have to be who you are already. You must believe in your life's purpose, that God crafted *you in particular* for extraordinary influence. You have to be certain that God intended you to fly on strong, golden wings. Do you believe that?

My senior year in high school was the first time I heard the term *plus model* on my favorite TV show. I adored watching Tyra Banks host *America's Next Top Model* and was enamored of watching the models compete in creative competitions to create the most flawless photos. Something in me said, "*That's* what I want to do with my life." I began to research and pursue how to make my heart's goal happen. One day I sat at the computer and sent out submissions to the top agencies in Chicago including Elite Model Management.

Elite's website advised me to not expect to hear from them for weeks because they receive thousands of submissions. The competition for the modeling industry is stiff. It takes them weeks to sift through all the submissions. So I was flabbergasted to receive a call back as soon as I sent my submission. I also knew in my heart of hearts that this was God's doing. What was He planning in my life through this wild opportunity? Part of me trusted that; the other part of me feared the worst.

I woke up the morning of the meeting excited and nervous. *Prepare yourself for a no*, I thought. *It's rare to even meet face-to-face with these people, but I bet it will be a no.* My insecurities were having a field day.

I had asked Lexie, my most fearless friend, to help me navigate Chicago traffic. Coming from poky little Adrian (well, it *is* poky compared to Chicago), I was intimidated by the thought of Chi-town rush hour.

Adventurous Lexie was game from the word "go." We started out early that morning on the four-hour trek to meet my destiny.

"When you come out of that agency with your contract we are going to *celebrate*!" Lexie exulted.

By nature, Lexie is the most happy-go-lucky, positive, rose-colored-glasses kind of girl you could ever hope to meet. I needed her glass-half-full attitude that day as my nerves jangled inside.

"I don't know, Lex...I mean, I am *hoping* but most likely I won't get a contract," I said. I just didn't want to be too disappointed if nothing happened. Have you ever been thrilled to death about something, but tried hard to stuff those feelings in a "probably not" box? Yeah, we all do this. It's a protective mechanism.

I will never forget that day as long as I live. Not just because I lost my phone at a rest stop, found it again, only for it to be stolen from a restaurant later on. Not just because my car mirror broke off after hitting a pole as my friend drove my car. And not because I accidentally allowed the keys to Lexie's dad's brand-new SUV to fly out the window while I was trying to take a picture of a rainbow (hey, it was an amazing rainbow!).

It's memorable because I thought what happened that day would finally mean *I meant something*. I thought the events of that day would be enough to make me feel complete.

Kasia, the agent with Elite Model Management who reached out to me after my submission, was the kind of girl you see sitting in the front row of the Dior spring fashion show in Paris. Elegant. Urbane. Even though I was extremely nervous, meeting Kasia and the other Elite agents was a relief: I had harbored a fear that a modeling agent would be like someone from the movies, a harsh, snobby, judgmental lunatic. But everyone was kind as they walked me around the room to meet each agent, took my measurements, and scanned me head to toe looking at my hair color, teeth, skin, body, etc. (Now I know what horses go through.) It was a strange feeling to have someone visibly and audibly evaluate my looks. I was being considered for their *Figure* division of plus-size/curve models.

"Ashley, go ahead and get changed back into your clothes and we'll talk." I had changed into a simple tank top and jeans for their appraisal. Inhaling deeply, I went to change, trying to prepare myself for whatever the verdict might be.

They were all smiling when I came out.

"Ashley, we would like to offer you a contract and welcome you to the Elite family." The Elite *family*? Sweet Mother of Pearl! I think I lost every sense I had. Briefly I wondered if I could be dreaming. Would I wake up back in my bed, slapping the snooze button?

But I was awake. They handed me my contract to look over and we began going over next steps. I would come to the agency to take a few lessons on posing and walking. I would need to color my hair back to brown and remove any highlights. I would need to invest in certain items to fill a model bag such as beauty products and clothing to take with me on jobs. Everything from teeth whitening products, eye depuffing products, hair extensions, and even body padding to change my body shape if needed! The agents stressed the importance of always being prepared.

I wandered out of Elite, into the Chicago sunshine in a stupor. I finally found Lexie, who was not one bit surprised that we were, in fact, going to have that celebratory dinner I had thought just hours earlier was so farfetched.

The rest of the day was horrible, from the stolen phone to the lost keys for the brand-new Envoy. When we got home, my car would not start, and I spent the night alone in an apartment, which I had been in the process of moving out of. No phone, no car, and a single mattress in the middle of the living room, ready to be hauled out. Also, I was flat broke. Yet I was deliriously happy. I had in my possession a contract that made me feel like everything was going to be all right. I had proof in black and white that I, chubby, unseen, run-of-the-mill Ashley Reitz was not only okay or good enough but elite. Once again, I had placed all my emotional eggs, all my purpose, meaning, and approval, in one basket, this time in the hands of Elite Model Management. I had no idea what adventures would come my way, but I was ready.

Like homecoming, I had placed my need for affirmation, purpose, and worth in the wrong hands—a modeling contract. As great as Elite was, no human hands can hold the weight of our need for significance. No human achievement or relationship can define us.

Listen, it's okay to be thrilled when we reach a longed-for goal! Have fun. Celebrate! As long as we ultimately remember who we are. Even though I had a modeling contract, I was missing out on God's purposes for me. Like homecoming, I quickly felt undeserving. In no time, I was wrestling with self-doubt and a sense of not belonging. I was thrashing, chicken-like, only able to fly a few feet in the air before tumbling back to reality.

It would be years before I would finally get it: Only God can define me. Only my Father can confer a profound sense of meaning in my life. Only God can transform me into an eagle.

Now Esther? She was an eagle, not a chicken.

"Yes, of course she was an eagle, Ashley," you might be huffing. "She was spectacular looking, so of course she flew on strong, golden wings! Why wouldn't she?"

I used to think the same thing about Esther, summing up the story this way: "Super-pretty girl gets chosen simply because she's super pretty." (Um, shallow!)

She then goes to a palace to get more pretty before she is brought to a king to see if she is pretty enough to be his queen (double shallow). But if we are only getting that out of the story, we are missing the slow boat to Babylon in a big way.

We get so focused on the "Esther was gorgeous" story before the actual "Esther was brave and faithful" story. We think at first that the story is fixated almost too much on Esther's looks. But her looks have a purpose.

Of course, it's impossible to verify her exact looks, but we are told she was plucked from a nationwide "Hottest in the Land" contest. I am picturing a bunch of Victoria's Secret models, all vying to be queen.

I imagine Esther (and them all) with fabulous naturally long lashes resembling the finest mink lash extensions. She had flowing, silken hair begging for a spot in a Pantene commercial. And her body was perfect in the way that swimsuit cover models' bodies are perfect.

She joins the other flawless ladies at the king's palace for a year of beauty treatments. Can you imagine being preened and primped and fluffed and fussed over for 365 days? Most of us would give anything for one solid day at the spa! The end goal was to be paraded by King Xerxes, who would then make his top selection. He would choose the most alluring, exceptional woman as his queen consort. He would say, "Will you accept this rose?" except the rose came with a kingdom.

"Wait, wait, wait...What does this have to do with me? Listen," you might be huffing again, "if I were given a year's worth of facials and seaweed wraps, nail treatments, and hot stone massages, at the end of the year I'd still be me, with stupendous toenails. In all reality, if King Xerxes was using a current dating app he would take one look at me and swipe left."

Hang on, there, pal. I promise it will be worth it.

Because Esther's story is for every girl who wears an invisible crown of righteousness, placed there by her Father. It's for the outwardly lovely. It's also for you if you shine with the kind of loveliness that isn't usually appreciated by our looks-obsessed world. Esther's story is for anyone who has ever wondered why God put them on His green earth. It's for me and for you.

The Bible tells us that it was no contest—Esther blew away the competition. Esther's pull on him was magnetic, and he "set a royal crown on her head and made her queen" (Esther 2:17).

She went to King Xerxes as herself, comparatively unadorned, simple, authentic. I believe her inner beauty was just as crucial as her outer beauty. She was humble, down to earth, and unselfish. King X was enthralled with what he could not see. Part of me wonders if the king was sick of seeing flashy girls, falling all over themselves and grabbing for status and wealth. Esther was different, wonderfully so. So smitten was Xerxes that he made the girl formerly known as Hadassah his queen and threw a huge party in her honor.

Here's where things get even more dramatic. Esther's cousin Mordecai, who had basically adopted her after her parents died, found out that there was a plot to assassinate the king. When Esther alerted the king, Xerxes's trust in her increased. Then Mordecai learned that Haman, the king's chief adviser, was plotting a genocide against all the Jews in Babylon, and that Haman had manipulated the king's consent to it! When Mordecai rushed to tell Esther, she wavered a little bit, worried about what the king would do when he found out she was Jewish. Plus, he hadn't asked for her in a month, and to approach the king uninvited was to risk her life. Esther was understandably scared.

And then her cousin said something that changed the course of human history. In one of the most poetic biblical passages, Mordecai speaks of God's purposeful timing: "Who knows but that you have come to your royal position for such a time as this?" (Esther 4:14).

She decided to go for it—"if I perish, I perish" she says (v. 16), not in a fatalistic way, but with deep obedience. That's how devoted she was to God's purposes in her life.

Submissive to her Maker, Esther also showed incredible wisdom. She asked Mordecai to get all the Jews, all her fellow God-followers, to fast and pray for three days. She and her lady's maids would be doing the same. Esther needed direction. She needed to know what she should do next. When we need God's guidance, prayer opens the doors for spiritual growth, removes distractions, and places us on a path to humility. At the end of the three days, she was ready to step into her elite purpose. Fueled by prayer, filled with wisdom, Esther bravely faced the king and ended up saving her people, the Jews, from mass slaughter. To this day, Jews celebrate Purim every March to remember a young woman's heroism.

Esther is definitely one of my heroes. There are so many takeaways from her story:

- She humbled herself and made sacrifices to spend time with the Lord. He revealed His ways to her. The same thing will happen when we humble ourselves, and pray for wisdom and courage. One of my favorite verses is Psalm 138:3: "When I called, you answered me; you greatly emboldened me."

- Esther was placed in a royal position to assist in the delivery of God's divine plan. How have you been placed in your own royal position to assist in the delivery of God's plan? ("Wait a little minute," you are grumbling. "I live in a trailer park. I work at *Walmart*! There's nothing remotely 'royal' or 'elite' about my 'position.'" I know, dear reader. I get it. Seems like a big stretch. But as a daughter of the King and a member of the "royal priesthood" of all God-followers, you are just as royal as Esther, Queen Elizabeth, and the Duchess of Cambridge,

spiritually speaking. And make no mistake—
your purposes on this earth are elite.)

- At first, Esther has her own plan (to avoid potential catastrophe by just not telling Xerxes about
Haman's plot). Luckily for humankind, she had
a change of heart, depended deeply on God, and
allowed Him to be her Life Planner. Reminds
me of one of my favorite verses: In her heart
a woman plans her course, but the Lord determines her steps" (see Prov. 16:9).

- God used Esther's beauty for a purpose, to get
her foot in the door. But her inner beauty won
the king over, ultimately. Her inner beauty saved
her people! Do you believe God also has a plan
for your appearance?

"God gave Esther everything she needed, physically, to accomplish his purpose for her life," says
blogger Heather Creekmore. "God had a mighty purpose for her life, and to fulfill that purpose, Esther
needed to look a certain way."[15]

God didn't make a mistake with Esther, and He
didn't make a mistake where He has you today. He
didn't make a mistake in the way He made you look.
"I think one of the most freeing lessons we can derive
from Esther is that God created each of us with a purpose," says Creekmore. "And, in this, he created the
way each of us looks, physically, with a purpose as
well."

We so often try to figure out where God wants us
to be or wish we were somewhere else. We wish we
looked like someone else. Esther and Leah's stories
teach us to let God do something with our life where

we *are*, while waiting for more to come. How do we reconcile His choices in the way He crafted us to look? We take a page from Esther's book and we pray, *God, why did You make me this way, with this lumpy body and acne and ugly, frizzy hair?* And the God who said, "You are not a mistake, my darling" will speak to you with so much love. "My daughter, My royal girl—I created you for elite purposes. I formed you, feature by feature, and said, 'It is good.' I shaped every cell in your body and called them exceptional. I whispered to your heart, 'Will you accept My love?' and planned your steps carefully 'for such a time as this.' I made you to soar, to mount up with wings like eagles."

The goals of this world may feel good—even amazing—for a time, but they deliver a short-lived satisfaction. When you realize you were pursued by a King for your singular purpose, your elite reason for being, you take another step into your story of freedom.

Be who you already are!

Because you, my friend, belong to the sky.

Beauty Box

1. When Ashley gets the call from Elite, she thought her modeling contract would "solve the question of my worthiness." Have you ever thought something or someone would answer the question of your worthiness?

2. Ask yourself, "Into whose hands have I placed my sense of meaning?"

3. "I knew that at my school I belonged everywhere and nowhere, which is an empty feeling." Have you ever felt that way?

4. Are you living your life as a chicken or an eagle? Are there any ways that you see yourself as a lowly barnyard chicken and are not aware of your potential grandeur? You could soar like an eagle. What would that look like for you?

5. Is it hard for you to believe that, as God's daughter, you are royal and chosen? Where do you think you have been placed right now to assist in the delivery of God's plan? How do you think God might use you?

6. When you feel unsure of God's mighty purposes in your life, repeat the following verse: "Perhaps this is the moment for which you have been created" (see Esther 4:14).

7
STRIVE

*A*re you trying your best to measure up—yet you still feel as if you're not enough, that you'll never be enough?

You are not alone.

The quest for perfection in our world is crazy-making—and endless.

Every day there is something new to chase after, some new look, weight, answer, thing, or person. And we wonder all the while, *Why am I so imperfect?*

But we get on that treadmill—literally and figuratively—and go after perfection anyway, because there's always...

- a fresh trend to try;
- a new diet to implement;
- an innovative product to buy; or
- a trendy "it girl" to emulate.

There will always be something to strive for or someone to strive to be. And it feels like a whole lot of pressure, doesn't it?

As middle and high school students, we strive to be popular among our peers by being whoever it is we think they want us to be. In college, our ideas change a little bit but we struggle for perfection in other ways. We still want to be seen as beautiful and smart, but as young adults the pressure comes from other sources as we try to establish our places in the world. As a young married person, we attempt to keep up the façade of a perfect love story. We want our relationship to be admired. And then as young moms we try so hard to keep up the impression that we are faultless mothers of flawless children. And so it goes. The phases of our lives change but the desire for perfection does not.

Mostly, we want *others to think* we have an ideal life, an existence that appears to be coming together nicely. It's all about what others think of us, even though *we know* we're far from perfect.

Another thing that doesn't change? The pressure and the feeling of discontentment. The world tells us, "When you've got it all together and every aspect of your life is impeccable, *then* you'll be happy."

The enemy hums in our ears, "You won't be free until you prove to everyone that you are important. You won't be fulfilled until you have every scrap of your junk under control. You won't be content and at peace unless you find a way for everyone to like you." Proven, controlled, and most of all, liked.

And we listen to the enemy buzzing in our ears instead of the still, small Voice in our souls. We lunge for the brass ring, over and over, but we never quite catch it. It's a never-ending feeling of being pushed and prodded, urged on to the next pursuit.

But our Father invites us into a different life, one in which our souls spill over with peace and gladness. Because running after our culture's next idea of perfect is a burden we were never meant to bear. You and me? We were crafted to travel lightly, carrying burdens only the size of, say, a medium-weight tote bag. Instead, we find ourselves crushed under the weight of a steamer trunk we were never supposed to pick up.

How do we begin to lighten our load? First things first: We need to be at peace with what we cannot change.

What a slog it is to drag through life fighting the things we cannot change. And there are so many things we cannot change.

One of the first battles I fought to be perfect—besides my weight—was my height. It seems so silly now because there is nothing a person can do to alter how tall they are. Yes, I can buckle up some four-inch Jimmy Choo heels and add a few inches, but there's no way to *subtract* inches, short of slouching like crazy.

I grew up one of the taller girls among my peers. Oh, I hated it at the time. At 5 feet 9 I was not a giant but I was quite a bit loftier than most of the girls my age growing up. The popular girls were petite, dainty little things who stood about 5 feet 2, tops, on their size 6 feet.

As a kid who didn't look outside of my small bubble of a world, that was my reality. I felt too tall. Too big! *Small is perfect, big is imperfect.* That was the message I received or perceived at my little Christian school.

You know what's funny? The things we often dislike about ourselves are the exact things that God gives us to accomplish His special intentions. It goes back to our elite purpose, as we just talked about in chapter 6.

Little did I know, when I was fruitlessly hunching over in school, that I would need to be a minimum of 5 feet 8 inches tall in order to even be considered model material. Most agencies turn you away if you're a smidgen under that height. In fact, many times I was turned down from jobs because I was "too short." Ha! Me? Too short?

Concurrently, I was fighting the battle of the bulge. As you already know, I also wanted to change my body. I desperately wanted to change my body! I agonized over the size of my chest and hips (and so on and so on). But all of the "flaws" I despised were 100 percent *why* I was chosen to begin my career with that agency! Had I been 5 feet 2 with small feet and slim little hips I would have been laughed out the door at Elite.

God works in mysterious ways, His wonders to perform. What I hated about myself as a child and teen were the exact reasons I was able to travel His appointed path! What do you dislike about yourself now? Is it something you can—or should—change or is it something with which you need to make peace?

Most of us know the Serenity Prayer:

God grant me the serenity
to accept the things I cannot change;
courage to change the things I can;
and wisdom to know the difference.

In other words, "God, help me be content and at peace with the way You have made me. If there are things to work on, let's work on them together. Give me Your boldness and wisdom to do what You would have me do. And *for the love*, help me figure out the difference between a tote bag and a steamer trunk."

Speaking of killing ourselves over something we

cannot change, the modeling industry is the slog of slogs when it comes to striving to be perfect. It is not exactly a business known for body image serenity!

One struggle I've witnessed countless times is when a plus/curve/figure model tries to go straight size or high fashion. Let's say a girl who is a size 10 is kind of in between those body categories and needs to drop down to a size 4, or more preferably a size 2, in order to stay in the modeling industry. For most women, asking them to drop from a 10 to a 2 is akin to demanding they drop eight inches in height. Some bodies are truly, naturally made to be *high fashion* thin. But most are not and to get that way requires strenuous work.

Now, it can be done. I've seen it done. But at what cost? Some models fluctuate from curve modeling to straight-size modeling, but they don't do it more than once or twice. Most come to realize, after staggering effort, that their body type cannot maintain that extremely low weight. They are utterly done in by the trying, the striving, the slaving at the gym three times a day. Their bodies—and spirits—simply were not designed to subsist on a fraction of calories needed to borderline function. You know, *function*. Exist. Blink. Breathe. Wave. And these poor girls collapse under the weight of it all, ironically in a mad bid to be lighter.

It *is* unhealthy to starve yourself for a possible (lucrative) paycheck. But we've all been there in some way. We've all pretended, performed, and tried to prove ourselves in unhealthy ways. I have pretended I had it all together when I didn't. I've played the role of the "good Christian girl." I've tried in so many ways to prove myself to others.

I'm betting you have too.

For a model, the "carrot" dangling just in front of her nose might be a size 2 body, but what's your carrot? You know the old carrot and stick metaphor, right? Based on the reward of a carrot and the punishment of using a stick to encourage a horse to move. A company might use a carrot and stick—more money is the carrot, loss of your job is the stick. Get it? Our enemy definitely uses this—more "enoughness" is the carrot, loss of "enoughness" is the stick.

When you look at your life and how you spend your time, what kinds of unhealthy pursuits are you hooked on? Name your carrot. How is Jesus better?

I think I speak for us all when I say we could use more serenity and less stress. More rest and less pressure. More authenticity and less pretending. The enemy wants us flattened like a bug on the road by all our striving, but our Father made us to stand tall—rested and strong in Him.

One way to make peace with your "dislike-ables"—aka the things we cannot change? Know that they make you more relatable to others. They really do!

I spent years mired in insecurity over my weight, my height, and—just keeping it 100 percent real—my lifelong self-doubt about math and anything math related. Of course this was intensified when I was in school, and I actually had to wrestle down those terrifying math problems on a daily basis. Just thinking about it makes tiny beads of sweat form on my upper lip, like an anxiety mustache (pretty, right?).

If you were to pose this question, "Ashley, would you rather take a math test and have your score published or skydive out of an airplane right now?" my reaction would be instant: "Pass the parachute!" (I don't know why you would ever ask me that terrible question, but let's just suspend our disbelief and pretend you are a mean math teacher with an airplane revved up on a runway nearby.)

My struggle with anything math (and this still includes figuring out a tip, y'all) made me sensitive to others. When I saw someone in school struggling with writing a paper or doing something I could more easily do, I was quick to encourage them and help them. Because of my insecurities about weight, height, math, and so on, I can more easily pick up on other people's discomfort and anxiety. My struggles make me want to cheer them on. It's like that verse, "What Satan meant for your harm, God meant for your good" (see Gen. 50:20). Our redeeming Father wastes nothing, including our weaknesses. He says, "That pile of your weaknesses, insecurities, and flaws? The world may see a heap of mud, but I see compost, rich and nourishing, able to grow you into your beautiful self."

Maybe you aren't happy about some traits God has given you, but I encourage you to start looking for the beauty and purpose in them. Pray and ask your Father to show you how He is transforming your insecurities into areas of strength and growth. Instead of bashing yourself over a stumble, ask God to open your eyes to opportunities for relating to people.

Try this prayer: *Okay God, You have made me the way I am for a reason. How can I best use my weaknesses and insecurities for You?* Praying this way has opened many doors of friendship and opportunities for encouragement. In God's economy, our weaknesses make us tender and watchful for others who need a boost.

Our imperfections *do* make us more authentic, which is ironic. Why? Because authenticity is the enemy of perfectionism. Authenticity—that is, being real—fights our flawed need to be flawless. And as much as we doggedly run after perfection and the desire to prove, prove, prove we are enough, we also crave the raw and the real.

Nate Ruess from the band Fun was once a guest mentor on *The Voice*. Nate listened intently as one of the contestants belted out a visceral yet technically unrefined song in rehearsal for the battle round of the show. This contestant didn't have purely powerful pipes or Juilliard-worthy intonation, but what they *had* was more valuable: Authenticity.

"I'd rather be moved than impressed any day," he said. The show's judges also praised the singer for her genuine delivery, and a relatable "stand in her shoes" performance. She wasn't trying to be someone she wasn't, and it made all the difference in her piece. All who heard her were moved, stirred by her vulnerability and lack of artifice.

I once heard the saying, "Vulnerability is the conduit of grace."

Openness—standing in our own shoes, being who God made us to be—is literally a channel to grace, a means to mercy.

When we stop pretending and performing, other people notice and feel more relaxed with us. They sense they can stand in *their* own shoes and be who God made them when they are in our company. Psalm 42:7 says, "Deep calls to deep." It doesn't say, "Fake calls to fake." We are wired to respond with open hearts when others lay down the pretense of perfection. God calls us out from our "perfect" hiding spots, and our authenticity calls out to authenticity in others.

I think most of us would agree with Nate Ruess—we'd rather be moved than impressed. If that's true, why do we pretend, perform, and fight to prove ourselves perfect?

I distinctly remember when I hit a wall in my early twenties. These thoughts dominated my mind: *All this running and trying so hard is exhausting. I am so tired, so weary. God, help me change so I can have some peace in my life!*

Before I hit the wall, I had been accepted into the running for the Miss Michigan pageant. No pressure there, right? Yeah, wrong. A new and intense goal was born. As I was unknowingly lugging around tons of body image and "enoughness" baggage, I tracked after that goal relentlessly. I filled out the extensive forms. I wrote mini essays on what was important to me and why I wanted to compete for Miss Michigan. I cited my height and weight, etc.

Ummm, about my weight…

I knew, unofficially, I had to get down to a certain weight if I wanted a chance to advance any further. Oh, they never come out and say, "You have to be a skinny size," but I was all too aware that not one of the previous winners had been above a size 2.

So of course, my body perfection campaign kicked into overdrive. Any beauty pageant contestant knows the drill all too well. It's just part of the gig. I had been working closely with a doctor and a trainer, and was almost to the point where I felt I could make it, weightwise.

And then I crashed.

I had raised my support, declared my running to all my friends and family, and studied like crazy. On the surface, I had laudable goals. I had been studying politics, current events, and human trafficking, which was a "new" subject back then. At the time, most people didn't realize that there was a thriving sex trade in our country and around the world.

I was going to stand up for victims and be a voice for them. I also wanted to be a body positive activist (while still figuring it all out myself). Those were worthy causes, and I wanted to have that pageant platform from which to advocate for them.

Also, if I'm being honest, I did not want to end up like one of those poor, nervous girls who, after being asked a question on live television, butchered the answer.

(For example, one beauty contestant in 1992 was asked, "Why are you proud to be an American?" She answered, "We are truly the land of the great. From the rocky shores of…Hawaii…to the beautiful sandy beaches of…Hawaii…America is our home." I could totally see myself saying something similar—"We are truly the land of the great. From the rocky shores of…North Dakota…to the beautiful sandy beaches of…Kansas…America is our home.")

Part of my goal was genuinely to represent health, to show anyone watching that a "beauty queen" could have a more average body weight. But as hard as I trained I knew I couldn't hang with those girls in the winner's circle. The strain was grinding my soul down to a nub. Somewhere in the middle of my two-a-day workouts, careful calorie journaling, and timing of what and when I ate, I dropped midchase. Suddenly I wanted nothing to do with the competition.

Before, I had dearly wanted the chance to prove I was good enough to compete for a title like Miss Michigan. After all, wouldn't a title like that prove my worth once and for all? But I was running on fumes. I got so worn down from the mental pressure to have a perfect body that I dropped out last minute.

Honestly, on some level I knew I was trying to fill up that hole inside. I believed that the label "beauty queen" would make me "enough." The enemy whispered that freedom would be found if I proved to the world—through a Miss Michigan win—that I was perfect. I bought into the lie. I believed two things at once—that I *could* be perfect by trying hard enough, and that I was far from perfect.

It was humiliating to drop out, but I was finished. I was done. Boy, did it ever sting to return the checks I had collected for the support. I hated to let people down, but I knew I couldn't keep going. Striving, struggling, and straining had propelled me toward that wall, and left me as a crumpled heap on the floor.

Have you ever found yourself there, on some floor, somewhere? That's...

- where we end up when we allow ourselves to be chased by a constant sense of inadequacy;
- where we arrive when we drink a big ole gulp of guilt with our morning coffee;
- where we land when we're going full throttle with our heads down, intent on perfection, instead of up, at Him—at the Perfect One.

We miss so much, don't we? He is there, you know. On the floors of our lives. When we crash, He's there to gently pick us up in strong arms and carry us to a place of rest and peace.

Unfortunately, most of us don't rest for long, do we? We don't stay connected to the Source of all peace and rest. We get restless looking for that next bandage to cover our flaws. We get up and start pushing ourselves all over again.

In the wake of my canceled mission to be Miss Michigan, I realized some things. The whole experience was just another version of me trying to be satisfactory in the eyes of others. I put disgusting pressure on myself to be better, to be more.

I was so unnecessarily hard on myself. My parents noticed.

"Ashley, you are the most confident insecure person," they said to me more than once. Confident *and* insecure? Pretty contradictory, right? Yet it was how I lived my life for so long. I knew God was love, but I didn't accept it. I knew He was enough, but I didn't believe it. I knew my Father offered rest, but I couldn't rest, not when I had fifteen pounds to offload, a husband to find, and a sparkly crown to earn.

I didn't know that it was okay to say, "You know what? I'm not enough, but that's okay, because Jesus is."

I still believed that I needed to be more perfect in order to be acceptable to God, others, and my someday husband.

I look back and see that I was captive to the quest. It owned me like a slave. And when we're owned by the pursuit of perfect, we are possessed by a whip-cracking slave driver with no compassion.

So let me ask you—who or what owns you right now? Is it...

- the gym?
- your diet?
- a guy's approval?
- someone's admiration?

The Father says, "Come back to me and I will give you rest."

Are you ready to stop striving and start resting in who God made you to be?

One of the very best ways is found in these eleven words: *I am me, and she is she, so let it be.* Yes, I'm talking about vanquishing the comparison demon.

You know all about my soul-crushing struggle with body image. Having a sister who literally could not gain weight if she tried did not help. It was probably one of most straining and draining aspects of my desire to have a perfect body. Because she did. Because she does. To this day.

Let me just say I love her immensely; Lauren is one of my closest friends. We are so much alike. Goofy, silly love-balls—that's us. She's my favorite person to laugh with and share my secret stories with. I just all around adore the girl.

Obviously, I felt like I had to give a disclaimer before I appear to hate on her. Ha!

Truly though, this girl has never worked out a day in her life, eats like a doggone 300-pound trucker, and has never agonized over not fitting into a pair of pants, a dress, a bathing suit…I could go on, but why torture you, my readers?

Growing up, I can't even tell you how many times I got seriously grouchy at home over this issue.

"What in the world is going on here?" I would complain to my parents. "If Mom makes fettuccine Alfredo and Lauren and I eat the same amount of the same meal, I gain and she goes negative!"

"Lauren can eat three donuts and not gain a pound, but I smell a donut and boom! The scale goes up."

My parents were pretty great about it. They gave me the best answer they could.

"Honey, that's Lauren and you are you," they would say, kindly. "You are taller. You are built different. You are simply different people. Don't compare yourself." They were totally right, of course. Though at the time I had a hard time absorbing their wise words into my skewed soul.

I kept trying to be perfect—as perfect as I thought Lauren was. Every time I did compare myself to her, another piece of my heart shriveled up. It ground me down to see my sister—someone who supposedly inherited the same DNA as me—effortlessly get what I wanted: a thin body. The more I compared myself to Lauren, the more she became my rival, not the sister I loved. I was engaging in a constant contest—how do I measure up? And it increased my self-induced pressure exponentially. I didn't get it then—that I could kill myself trying harder and doing more, but I would *never* be Lauren. Why? Because I was someone else!

Such a simple concept, yet I failed to grasp it for eons.

I am me, and she is she, so let it be.

For years, I couldn't *let it be*. And it hurt me—and one of my most sacred relationships.

Thankfully, as I began to allow the Father to heal my innermost being by spending time with Him and soaking in His approval and love for me, my shrunken heart expanded and grew. I realized I had a choice. I could choose to obsess about all the things Lauren and others had that I didn't have, but the cost would be high. We can go absolutely bonkers with jealousy and inadequacy, can't we?

It's tempting to put naturally thin ladies (or those I perceived as being naturally thin) in a box and go crazy thinking about how easy they have it.

Meanwhile we conveniently forget that everyone struggles with something. Everyone has something that tears them up in the middle of the night.

I am me, and she is she, so let it be.

How do we plant that into our hearts? How do we stop the cycle of comparison? We pray and ask God to open up those tiny little boxes and let the real image bearers come out. Human beings, shaped by a loving Creator. We ask Him to help us see our rivals through His eyes. We remember that every human being in our fallen world is carrying something heavy. We thank God again for making us who we are—women who belong to Him. And we repeat this line again and again until it sticks: *I am me, and she is she, so let it be.*

We can also counteract perfectionism—"the disease to please"—with healthy habits. Seek wholesome ways to be *who you are already* in Christ—holy, kept, and loved.

This is key: Include the Father in your every pur-

suit. Check in daily to see if you're in balance. Whatever a health regimen means to you—vegan + yoga,
high protein + Zumba, a sensible diet + walks—talk it
all over with the One who is pleased to call you His
girl. Make sure you check in spiritually about other
"regimens" and pursuits—academic, social, beauty-
related, etc. Are you living authentically, in good balance, or are you about to hit a wall?

One of the healthiest habits I've ever incorporated
into my life is holy self-talk. When I'm harried and
feel undone by life, I am a huge fan of speaking truth
out loud: "I am a daughter of the King! God, You love
me and made me special! I know You have good for
me regardless of how I feel right now! You are enough.
Period."

Challenge yourself to *divest* from whatever makes
you strive and *invest* in authentic you. Dedicate time
to prayer and seeking your Father's face. Make it your
goal to know and love Jesus, then watch what He does
in and through you. Fill up with the truth of your
identity in Him. Step off the treadmill and take a deep
breath.

Here's the truth: God *can't* love us more based on
our performance. It's not in His nature. It's not how
He works.

"This is real love—not that we loved God, but that
he loved us and sent his Son as a sacrifice to take away
our sins" (1 John 4:10 NLT).

God is *not* in His heavenly tribunal, pronouncing us
worthy because of our efforts.

He's not saying, "That young lady is a real gem because she graduated top of her class or is making a
fortune or was on the front page of a prestigious mag-

azine or is a size 2." He is saying "*My* girl is a gem—and I love her more than she will ever know." But we just can't wrap our minds around a love like that.

God is the Creator and definition of beauty. He does not need your money. He does not need your ability or achievements. All those things add nothing to Him or to you, His glorious workmanship.

Leave your striving at the curb, sis.

Park your fears of letting people down.

Ditch the performing and the pretending.

Hand over your steamer trunk to the only One who can lug that thing around with ease. Better yet, just look up and say, "Take it." No need to heft that load even one more time.

Tune out the buzzing, and tune in to the Voice that says, "Come to Me, all who are weary and burdened, and I will give you rest."

You were built to depend on God, my friend, not yourself. You were made to travel lightly.

Beauty Box

1. How much does your current "luggage" weigh? Are you carrying a tote bag, a suitcase, or a steamer trunk? How can you unload your excess baggage on God today? And just for fun, what's your all-time favorite handbag or tote bag and why?

2. What do you dislike about yourself now? Is it something you can—or should—change or is it something you need to make peace with? Pray the Serenity Prayer and ask God for His peace and wisdom to fill you up.

3. When you look at your life and how you spend your time, what kinds of unhealthy pursuits have got you hooked? Name your carrot. How is Jesus better?

4. "Maybe you aren't happy about some traits God has given you but I encourage you to start looking for the beauty and purpose in them." What are some ways your weaknesses might actually be good, rich compost? Pray and ask God to show you how He is transforming your insecurities into areas of strength and growth.

5. Do you agree with Nate Ruess from Fun, when he says, "I'd rather be moved than impressed any day"?

6. Who or what owns you right now? Is it the gym? Your diet? A guy's approval? Someone's admiration? An achievement?

7. *I am me, and she is she, so let it be.* How do we stop the cycle of comparison? "We ask Him to help us see our rivals through His eyes." Who in your life do you need to pray this prayer about?

8
SLIDE

*H*ave you ever had a string of misfortune stretch out for so long you didn't know how much more you could take?

Unless you are an extraterrestrial, I am betting you have had such a rough period in your life. It doesn't even have to be the worst of the worst—the death of someone you love and can't bear to be without. Even a run of bad luck, when it seems that you can't get a win to save your life, can bring you down and cause you to question everything you believe in.

You're drained. Depleted. Questioning why God would allow bad things to happen to you, and then they happen again. When it rains it pours, and after a bad run, when we feel lashed by the downpour, cold and drenched, we need to remind ourselves of the Fire that burns inside. We need to remember that, no matter how far the slide, our Father still holds us. We are still safe and warm with Him.

I had a year in my life where I felt like I was sliding down a big hill, and no matter how hard I tried to get back on solid ground, things kept happening. And I kept sliding. Oh, it wasn't as bad as poor Britney's 2007. No mugs and T-shirts were made to commemorate my bad year—or your bad year, I bet. As opposed to Britney, when we have a very bad, terrible, no good year, we go through our troubles without paparazzi camped out in our yards and hanging on our cars. At least we didn't have our woes splashed across the headlines of every media outlet—so that's something to be thankful for, anyway.

During my bad year, I felt a little like Job's third cousin, once removed.

Let me just say this: Obviously, very few people have it as bad as Job. His ten children died—so the worst happened to him. I wonder, did the other terrible things—the loss of his home and wealth and getting horribly sick—pale in comparison? I bet they did. Even having his body covered in excruciating boils was probably like a drop in the bucket. His only relief was scraping his ulcers with shards of pottery.

I feel for his wife too. That much-maligned, unnamed woman lost her ten little loves too. Enough said. On top of that horrific loss, she went from being the richest lady in the region to having to beg for food at the city dump. No wonder she was angry at Job for not cursing God. Why have we always judged her so harshly?

So I am not comparing what I went through to what Mr. and Mrs. Job went through. Not even close. But still, believers throughout the centuries have looked to Job as a model of suffering. When a lot of things go wrong, we think of Job. When things went wrong in my life, that's who *I* thought of too.

After I dropped out of the Miss Michigan pageant, I experienced a long stretch where I just couldn't seem to get out of a rut. Several areas of my life crumbled. Worse, to me, was the fact that I had no control or ability to fix these things. For a girl in her early twenties, working so hard to make things come together and create a life for herself, it felt like I was slipping down a hill, grasping at rocks and clumps of dirt before the next setback would send me sliding further.

First, right before I dropped out of the pageant, a significant relationship fell apart. Breaking up, like the song says, is very hard to do. I cried buckets! How had this happened? I felt like Jeff and I made sense. I didn't have much to compare it to since he was my first serious relationship, but dating him made me feel like I was on track for that perfect life I craved. He had his own company, a great family, and wanted the same things as me—faith, family, a hardworking, wholesome kind of life. And then there was the House on the River. At the peak of the relationship, he showed me some houses he liked. "I want you to like this house because it'll be yours too someday."

Mine? I mean, *hello!* How do you tell a girl something like that without her planning a perfect little Pinterest board right on the spot? The relationship did move quickly, and at the time I was proud to say I had probably found my perfect match. (Key word: *proud.*) I was twenty-one, which in my community was not young at all to be at this stage. In fact, I was a bit behind the eight ball as far as snagging a man was concerned. Not quite an old maid but not a young maid either. A medium maid! At least that's how I felt.

I had been extremely intentional in my dating life, trying hard to only date husband material. Now I see something in all of that I didn't see at the time. I thought I had *control* over that area of my life. And control felt good.

Look, Lord! We did it! I am doing things the right way and this time next year, Jeff and I will be married (in your perfect timing!) and life will be simply grand.
"We." "Your." Yeah, right.

And then, without a whole lot of warning, the relationship into which I had placed all my hope dissolved in a moment. Jeff and I got into this huge disagreement, and neither of us handled it very well. Especially me. I wish I had handled things differently. Not that we would be together today, with two kids, a pet hamster, and a picket fence. That fight was a clue, though not all fights are. It was pretty clear we were not meant to get married after all. A wheel came off in my life.

The fairy tale went poof, and worse, my pride in what I thought *I* had created disintegrated into dust.

Goodbye, beautiful House on the River with children and pets frolicking in the yard!

See ya, ideal husband and perfect Christian marriage!

Cheerio, sensible, solid, "foolproof" life plan!

I not only ditched my dreams of building a life with Jeff, but in the wake of our breakup, all plans were scrapped for my future, period. *Where to from here?* I agonized. The neat, orderly path I thought I was traveling had hit a roadblock. Between my surprise breakup and dropping out of the pageant, humble pie was on my menu for quite a while.

Now I see that wasn't a bad thing at all. Oh, it hurt—bad. But God used those losses in my life. I lost control of things I had no business trying to control, and the façade fell apart.

Still twenty-one, a pageant dropout, and a "medium maid," I was shaken at these plot twists in my life, unsettled on another level. The loss of Jeff had created a hole at the center of my life. Who was I without Jeff in my life? What was my identity without the pageant goals to chase after? I was lonelier than ever.

Yet our redeeming, rescuing Father was at work within my new, unwelcome solitude. He is at work within *your* loneliness too. Calling, wooing, inviting us to new closeness with Him. Listen in, can you hear Him?

"Loneliness is meant to be an invitation to draw closer to God," says author Jennie Allen in *Nothing to Prove*. "But our tendency is to try frantically first to meet that need with people, to prove to ourselves we are lovable and funny and worthy of attention."[16]

Like most girls on the bitter end of a breakup, I doubted if I was lovable, funny, or worthy of attention. Have you ever felt the same way?

Jennie Allen also says, "When we begin to find our deepest, most fundamental needs met in God, then we will go from using people to meet our needs to enjoying people despite the ways they disappoint us."

I was using Jeff and the pageant to meet my needs. Today I know these losses were needed. They were essential for my growth.

I was at the very beginning of allowing God to meet my needs, with so much more to learn. I was just at the start of understanding how lovable and beautiful I was because of Jesus.

But that terrible year of being Job's cousin three times removed had just begun, and I still had a long way to slide.

I don't know if you have ever experienced the true gift of having family not officially related to you. Friends who are family in the truest sense. A bonus mom or dad, sisters and brothers, grandmas and grandpas. I hope so, because these people immeasurably enrich and elevate our time on this earth.

Growing up, our official family was best friends with our bonus family across the street. They became essential to us—to me. I literally knew them better and spent more time with them than my own extended blood family. They say blood is thicker than water. But water sometimes quenches a deeper thirst—a longing for community and belonging.

I belonged to the Harrison family and they to me. Since I was five years old they were among the most important and influential people in my life. At every age and stage of life they were there, even after we moved two and a half hours away to Adrian between my freshman and sophomore years. Their two girls were my best friends and we spent the majority of our time together. If we weren't walking to school together, we were playing outside at either home. If we weren't at home, we were at church together.

Kevin, my second dad, was always there for us. When our family had a house fire in the middle of the night, who came running across the street to rescue us? Kevin. When my car broke down and I needed someone to help me because my own dad was far away, who was there in a jiffy? Kevin. He was there with his truck when my sister and I needed help moving from our apartment, and on many other occasions when he could serve in some way. I had no doubt of his love for me.

I remember one time I was talking about where I would get married someday.

"I want to get married far away on some mountain-top somewhere," I had laughed. "No one will come because it'll be so far away!"

Kevin's response was as serious as it was sweet.

"*We* will," he said, pointing to his wife. "It doesn't matter where you get married. We wouldn't miss it."

Kevin also had a knack for knowing when I was down and needed to hear the world's best Donald Duck impression: "Boy, oh boy!" "What's the big idea, you widdle scamp?" "Scram!" "Phooey!" "Doggone!"

It was impossible not to giggle through his fake-angry quacking. The sun came out again after just a few spit-laden quacks. Kevin always knew how to make me feel like everything was going to be all right.

But then came the day when I got the terrible phone call from Michigan. And Kevin couldn't tell me what I wanted to hear. It was Tessa, Kevin's daughter, and she was screaming. There was loud crying in the background. Kevin had been killed in a motorcycle accident.

I was devastated on a personal level, and also for the much greater loss my friends were facing. They had lost their dad, too young. Seeing the people I loved most in the world hurting so much, and not being able to do much of anything to help, was unbearable.

Kevin's death was hard to process, as anyone who has lost someone knows. I began to understand just a small piece of how Job had felt. Kevin had most of his life ahead of him. He should have died in his bed at age ninety, surrounded by children and grandchildren. I was angry at God for allowing this tragedy. Didn't He know those girls needed their dad? I was confused, and my faith in a loving Father took a kick in the chops.

Maybe you've lost someone you love. I didn't say "loved," because there is nothing past tense about love. I'm so sorry. You must miss that person so much! Sometimes it can be hard to understand why God lets terrible things happen. Sometimes nothing makes sense.

One thing I do know is that it's okay to feel—to grieve and rage and cry and throw stuff if it makes you feel better. Death is not natural for God's creatures— we were not created for death. Yet it's a part of life in our sin-damaged world.

It's also okay to ask, *Why is this happening to me?* Job, for example, wanted clarity about his suffering. He asked God *why* no less than twenty-five times. *Why did you take my loved ones away from me?!* It's not a sin to ask God questions, even when we're yelling at Him. He can handle it. He made us to love deeply, and He knows more than anyone what our suffering feels like.

In his book *The Purpose Driven Life*, Rick Warren says the following about "venting" to God[17]:

> Genuine friendship is built on disclosure. What may appear as *audacity* God views as *authenticity*. God listens to the passionate words of his friends; he is bored with predictable, pious clichés. To be God's friend, you must be honest to God, sharing your true feelings, not what you think you ought to feel or say.

Ought to. Should. These are words that ought to be banned. They should be illegal!

How many times have we stuffed our true feelings in some good Christian girl box and told them to behave?

- A good Christian girl shouldn't feel anger toward someone else, no matter how badly that person hurt her.
- Someone with their act together can only grieve for a short, appropriate amount of time. It's not okay for you to mourn someone for too long.
- A person of faith ought to get over it / snap out of it more quickly than the world does. It's only right.

Truth flash: All of the above statements are utter nonsense.

We were made in the image of the One who turned the moneychangers' tables, the One who wept at Lazarus's grave. The One who let Job vent to his angry, broken heart's content, and then said Job was "righteous."

Job, as one of God's best friends, was real about his suffering. He spoke passionate words to his Maker, crying out for answers, and his honesty increased their closeness.

If you're underwater right now, drowning in sorrow, be honest with God. Ask Him to grant you peace of mind. He cares about your distress. Do you believe it?

Pay close attention to Job, who knew that God saw his grief and despair. Job resolved that the Almighty had a rescue plan for him. "I know that my redeemer lives," he declared in Job 19:25. Can we declare the same thing when we are in the deep pain of loss?

When Kevin died, I wish I had been more authentic. I wish I had believed that God cared about my pain and the much larger pain of my dear friends. I wish I, like Job, had resolved that the Almighty had a rescue plan for us all.

I could only see on the surface of things: Kevin's actual death, the decay of my relationship with Jeff, and the attached dreams. Even as things continued to fall apart in my life, I had no idea then that God was planting something critical in my soul.

Despite the disappointment I felt over dropping out of Miss Michigan and my breakup with Jeff, there was one area of my life that seemed to be thriving. My modeling career had fallen into place just as I had hoped it would. I was working full-time modeling and I traveled frequently to exotic places such as the Florida Keys, New York City, and all over Mexico. A successful modeling career made me feel like I was actually doing something special in the world.

What I didn't know then was that I was already doing something special in the world just by being the Father's daughter. Just by being who I already was. I still thought "special" status needed a whole lot of striving on my end.

I had worked with a national brand for years and loved the fact that we always had great locations in which to shoot, fun crews on set, and scads of exposure in both print and online advertisements and catalogs. I adored their cute clothing, and overall working for them was a dream gig. That summer in particular I worked a ton for them.

Even though my personal life was in shambles, my

professional life was pretty darn good. I was really trying to see the silver lining until the day the silver lining got tarnished. The phone rang with bad news: "I'm extremely sorry to tell you this," my agent said in a worried tone. Uh, *that* opening line never bodes well.

"I want you to know we have lawsuits started." *Gulp.*

"But basically, in a nutshell, [the brand you worked for] just sold the company and filed for bankruptcy." My heart dropped into my stomach. I braced for what I knew must be coming.

"You won't be getting paid for months of your work and there will be no reimbursement for all of your months of travel expenses."

My silver lining turned black overnight. In the modeling world you often don't get paid for months after you work a job. It's standard procedure. But I was expecting and depending on those paychecks.

I could hardly believe what had happened. The brand was big and well-regarded. All our clients are screened so that this kind of thing is not supposed to happen. But it did. With the last client anyone in the industry would have expected to go belly up. I shook my head with the irony of it all: I had actually turned down work from other brands so that I could work for this one!

Shortly after that bombshell, adding insult to injury, I had an accident that soaked up whatever savings I had. It was midnight and I was in downtown Chicago when the tie rod of my car snapped and catapulted me into the wall of a parking garage. Thankfully, I was unhurt but my car was a mess. Thousands of dollars of body work later, my little financial cushion lost all its feathers. A couple of months later, when some genius in a parking lot clipped off part of my fender and drove off without leaving a note, I just drove around with a busted fender. I was broke.

Ultimately the lawsuit my agency and others filed against the brand would settle on less than ten percent of what we worked for. Multiple agencies and many of my fellow models were bitterly unhappy about the outcome, but there was no other recourse. Financially, the rug had been ripped out from under me. Part of me knew God would provide. (Then again, God's provision was something I had never tested before in my life.) But part of me was rattled to the core as I lost control of my livelihood, my money. Why had this happened to me? I had done the work and done it well, yet my security had collapsed through no fault of my own.

A part of Job's suffering was money related. God allowed Job to lose pretty much every penny he'd ever earned. In today's terms, think of Mark Cuban or Bill Gates going from living in mansions and riding in limos to living in shelters and riding the city bus.

Job's money losses were staggering, far greater than any financial stress you or I will probably ever endure. But that doesn't mean it's not scary and stressful when we don't know how we will pay our bills.

Because we live in a world where companies go bankrupt, tie rods snap, and strangers ram into our cars in parking lots, we will all face financial setbacks, big and small, throughout our lives.

The Bible teaches us to "consider it all joy" when things go badly. Why? Because when our worlds are shaken, our checkbooks don't add up, and our bank accounts are dangerously low, that's when we are most likely to depend on God. He wants to take care of His girls (and guys too). He wants to be the One we turn to for our daily bread, not a job or an investment. He wants us to look up at Him and say, "There is no other way for me to make this work without Your help, Your provision."

May we remember His ever-present help in times of trouble—yes, that includes money trouble. Get outside under the big sky and remind yourself who your God is. Trust that if He can make and maintain the entire universe, surely He will sustain you.

Our Heavenly Father feeds the sparrows and clothes the lilies; He will take care of you and me.

I didn't think things could get worse after experiencing a breakup, giving up my dream, Kevin's death, and going broke, all within such a short time. Boy, was I wrong.

With a bad few months behind me, I decided I needed to get away. I moved down to a little island off Florida to escape and refocus. Palm trees and ocean breezes were doing their healing work, and I was beginning to feel optimistic again. Just as sparks of hope were flickering, I flew to Boston with a friend on a work trip to investigate the possibility of being involved in a salon business. *This will be a new start. This next phase of my life will be different*, I thought.

Yanking myself up by the bootstraps, I was determined to turn my situation around. *I am going to prove to myself and anyone watching that, despite these setbacks, I am a talented and confident young lady who has her life together. I will make something of myself. I will prove that I am worthy. Happiness and success—here I come!*

Weirdly, I sensed something off about this salon deal from the start. When Karina introduced me to her friends—and potential backers—I immediately felt out of place. They were all young, successful business owners of retail stores and restaurants who all appeared to spring forth from a long line of older successful business owners. Clearly, they were used to living a life of luxury and prominence. I fought my feelings of discomfort and tried my best to just roll with it.

After touring the city and the proposed business space for our salon, we went to dinner together and met a large group of *their* friends. I knew quickly I was out. The next day I would be flying back home. This business deal was not a fit for me. I had no intentions of ever returning. *Just smile and meet these people graciously and make it through the evening,* I thought. I didn't know then that making it through the evening would require every ounce of courage I had, not to mention heaven battling on my behalf.

I have always trusted my intuition, but I never would have suspected that my growing uneasiness was really a silent warning.

I felt my discomfort heighten at dinner. As soon as it was remotely polite to make my excuses, I made them. I had had enough of this group. On the surface, they all seemed pleasant enough. But arrogant, and quick to flaunt their wealth. Besides, I could not get past the feeling in my gut that something was not as it should be. I planned to make a quick stop at the condo where

Karina and I were staying and leave to spend the night in a hotel by the airport. I couldn't wait for my flight back to Florida.

It was here that things began to spiral out of control. Unbeknownst to me, one of the men in our group had slipped something into my single glass of champagne. I could feel myself fading even as I waited outside the restaurant for my ride to the condo. Suddenly, someone came up behind me and hit me hard on the shoulder. Startled and wincing, I turned around and saw a man who had been with the dinner group. I had been introduced to him but otherwise he was a stranger to me. What on earth had just happened? Despite my growing fogginess, panic rose. I knew I needed to get back to the condo, pack fast, and get out of there, away from him.

What I did not expect was for the whole group—including him—to go back to the condo where I was staying to hang out.

I prayed I could just quietly slip into my room, pack my bags, and escape before he noticed. But that didn't happen. Fighting this incredible disorientation, I fumbled around, throwing things into a suitcase. Out of nowhere, I was jumped by what felt like a giant bag of bricks. It was him. The man's arms were like steel beams as he closed me into a headlock.

Immediately my body went into a form of shock. I was shaking with fear as I wondered who this person was and what was going to happen.

My attacker was clearly on drugs and not fully aware of what he was doing. I struggled and tried as hard as I could to get away from him, but his hold on me was locked down. Was I about to be raped or even killed? There was a moment where I tried to create space between my neck and his arm so I could breathe better. I looked up toward the ceiling to plead to God.

"Lord, if You see me, please help me to get out of here safely!" My breath was ragged and my words choked. "Jesus. Jesus. Jesus. Please help me!" Even in those terrifying moments, it crossed my mind that this was not the sort of thing that happens to good Christian girls. *I'm the smart girl. I'm the safe girl. I'm the girl who avoids any situation where I could end up like this. So how am I here and how is this happening?*

I could not comprehend how someone like me could be in trouble this deep. I had no idea if I was going to live. I had no idea what he was capable of.

"Leave me alone! Leave me alone!" I pleaded over and over. He ignored my every cry and seemed to be proceeding to force himself on me. *This is happening. I am about to be raped. Oh God, why? Help me!*

And then he stopped. He just did. Muttering to himself incoherently, my attacker got up and walked out the door. Still dazed from the drug he had given me, I stumbled around the room, throwing my stuff haphazardly into my suitcase.

What just happened? Why didn't he rape me? Why? It was all I could think of. Relief drained into my blood vessels like morphine, and it was all I could do not to collapse. *Focus! Focus! You've got to find Karina and get out of here now!*

Why didn't I scream? Why didn't I run out of there and tell everyone that this monstrous man had just attacked me? I was in a state of posttraumatic shock, for one thing. Now I realize I was afraid of the group. My instincts told me they were not to be trusted. After all, the man was their friend. What would happen if I accused him of attacking me? The urge to get out of there was like none other.

As soon as I could, I found Karina and we left immediately. It was very early in the morning so we stayed at her family's house before heading to the airport. I told her what had happened. I showed her the bruises around my neck and body. And the look on her face scared me even more because I knew what had happened had been real.

Later that morning we called for a ride to take us to the airport as we sat with our bags. My brain had left planet Earth and was now circling the universe, looking for a safe place to land. My feelings—the ones I could register as such—zigzagged from profound gratitude for not being hurt worse and devastation over what had happened. It was a weird place to be, on the corner of relief and crisis. All I wanted was to get on a flight and go home.

Right before we were about to board our flight my phone rang. It was my mom. *Why would she be calling me now?* I thought. *She never calls me on Sunday right after church. Be calm. Act normal.*

I answered as steadily as I could. I did not want to have some sort of meltdown right there in the airport

"Hi, honey!" My mom's sweet voice just about broke me.

"I just had to tell you something neat that happened at church today. Norma Smith came up and asked me how you were doing. She said she woke up out of her sleep last night and God told her to pray for you!"

Goosebumps raised all over my arms. The image of dear, elderly Norma Smith popped into my head. She was frail of body but mighty and bold of spirit. Her prayers had saved me—that much was crystal clear. God had woken her up specifically to battle for me in my most vulnerable moment. He had heard me crying out to Him and He had protected me.

I hung up the phone without telling my mom what had happened. I had come close—especially after hearing about Norma's prayers—but the words simply would not come.

It would take me a long time to tell my loved ones about the attack. It would take me a long time to process the attack. But even in my darkest hour of memory, I held on to the fact that God had heard my prayer.

Suffering happens. No matter how much we try to prevent it, there's simply no way to avoid it. We try to control our circumstances, but things fall apart. Relationships crumble. People we care about die. Our finances go bust, despite our careful little nest eggs. And sometimes we are wounded terribly by our fellow human beings.

I am the kind of person who likes to have it all together. *Obviously.* I want to do what's right and I hate disappointing people. I also hate the idea of disappointing God. Every time something had gone wrong that year—from Miss Michigan to Jeff to my big client's bankruptcy, I had dug in my heels and tried harder to stop the falling. My feelings of inadequacy were stirred up by each setback, and my default was to kick my "get it together and you'll feel better" mode into overdrive.

So I got gritty. I got plucky. And I mustered all

my grit and pluck into moving forward. "Keep on truckin'," the bumper sticker on the semi says. I kept on truckin', baby! But none of that was one bit helpful after I was attacked.

I hadn't healed from any of what had happened before the attack. Not really. I thought I could manage by myself, without really bringing my Father into it any deeper than the surface level. Have you ever thought you could manage your troubles without God's help?

By submitting my will to God, I could have availed myself of His healing.

He is *Jehovah Rapha*—the God Who Heals. He longs to bind up our wounds and lay His healing hands on our broken places. After the attack, I was broken. My year-long slide had culminated in me lying there, fractured and bruised, with the kind of damage only God can repair. Quickly, I realized no amount of grit or pluck could save me now. Only God. And of course, I had to "heal the hard way" (more on that later).

We don't usually know why God sends trials into our lives, but we do know His plan is ultimately to grow us up for the better. To sharpen our understanding. At the end of the Book of Job, we see a stronger and more mature Job who grew in his understanding of God. He understood God's ways better, and built up confidence in God's nature. Job increased closeness with his Father.

Do we avoid suffering or cope with it in unhealthy ways? Or do we submit and allow healing to come, along with the possibility of new growth?

I love the planting metaphor Parker Palmer brings to the topic of suffering:

I am easily fixated on surface appearances—on the decline of meaning, the decay of relationships, the death of a work. And yet, if I look more deeply, I may see the myriad possibilities being planted to bear fruit in *some season yet to come.*

In retrospect, I can see in my own life what I could not see at the time: how the job I lost helped me find the work I needed to do, how the Road Closed sign turned me toward terrain I needed to travel, how losses that felt irredeemable forced me to discern meanings I needed to know. On the surface, it seemed that life was lessening, but *silently and lavishly the seeds of new life were always being sown.*[18] [emphasis added]

We, too, are easily fixated on the surface, on what *seems* to be happening. We give little thought to how today's troubles might actually bear fruit in some season yet to come. Don't forget your God is a God of justice. He will not let you go through a season of hardship and ignore your season of reward.

When things go wrong in our lives, we feel anything but beautiful. It seems as if hardship causes life to lessen, not increase. But is it possible that God has been planting seeds of beauty in our lives—silently and lavishly—all this time?

Beauty Box

1. Have you ever had a relationship break up? Hurts, doesn't it? How did you pick up the pieces and move on? What advice would you give a friend going through a bad breakup?

2. "Water sometimes quenches a deeper thirst—a longing for community and belonging." Have you ever had that thirst for community met through people who are not your official family? Take the time to drop a nonfamily family member a line of thanks today!

3. Have you ever felt like it wasn't okay to be angry at God? Angry at another person? Why or why not?

4. "If you're underwater right now, drowning in sorrow, be honest with God. Ask Him to grant you peace of mind. He cares about your distress." Do you believe it?

5. Money troubles can make us feel stressed, frustrated, and worried. What was the worst financial crisis you have faced? How did you see God take care of you?

6. When you are going through hardship, find encouragers! Surround yourself with good friends who will strengthen you in the Lord, not draw you away from Him. Thankfully, Job did have one encourager in his life, the unnamed pal who reminded him "God will not reject a blameless man.... He will yet fill your mouth with laughter, and your lips with shouting" (Job 8:20–21 ESV).

7. How did my account of the attack make you feel? Have you ever had anything like this happen to

you? The Justice Department estimates that one in five women will experience rape or attempted rape during her college years, and that less than five percent of these rapes will be reported. Healing may take months or years—there's no timetable. Here are some resources to help you navigate the process: rainn.org/recovering-sexual-violence. Call the National Sexual Assault Telephone Hotline at 800.656.HOPE to be connected with a trained staff member from a sexual assault service provider in your area.

9
CURVE

When life throws you curves, what do you do? You can let those hard and unexpected turns twist and bend you into someone brittle and hard, or you can yield to the God who can shape hardships into a turn for the good.

For me, the previous year had been terrible. I did not emerge unscathed from the negative turns my life had taken, especially the attack. Really, if you're human, you don't emerge unscathed. Nope—I was scathed, which is not a commonly used word, but it should be. Long after the physical bruises faded, the invisible damages were taking their toll. I did not have the first clue how to cope with trauma, and rather than seek healing, I shrank back into myself.

I had debated how to tell my family about the attack. I toyed with asking for counseling or something that would help me find some peace. The year had been so awful to begin with—and now this? Honestly, I was afraid that people would somehow blame me. This is what we do as women—blame ourselves. Experts say the vast majority of victims worry about somehow being blamed, and these assaults usually go unreported.

I knew in my heart I had done nothing wrong. But

would people believe me? Coming from a conservative background, I wondered if I should have had that glass of champagne. Did having alcohol play into my judgment that night? But of course, I knew in my brain that wasn't true. One glass would not affect my judgment, and the attacker could have slipped the drug into water or Diet Coke or even milk.

I was also embarrassed, even though I had done nothing about which to *be* embarrassed. I feared causing my parents hurt or distress. Would they force me to press charges? I just wanted the whole thing to disappear. I didn't think I could deal with any emotionally disturbing conversations—aka drama—on top of what had happened. Yet it kept nagging at me—I knew I needed to tell my parents.

One day I had carefully planned out what I would say and how I'd ask them for some prayer support. I called the house and my mom answered. Heart hammering, I prepared to launch into this dreaded conversation. My mom interrupted me.

"Oh! Honey, one minute before you start. Your dad is yelling from the other room that he has to say something first."

My dad picked up the phone from the other room.

"Hi, Shwee." (Don't ask me where I got that nickname but everyone in my family calls me that.)

"I just wanted to tell you how much I love you," he said in a tender voice. I could hear his speech break up a little, which was highly unusual for him. "I looked at a picture of you and your older sister today from when you were very little. You were in your tiny Easter dresses, wearing gloves and ruffly socks…"

He kept going. "I thought to myself, *How precious*

are they?! I love those little girls so much, and I don't want anyone to ever, ever hurt you!"

Well, honestly, how do you follow *that* up with "Dad, I was attacked"? I scrapped my plans to tell them everything. I teared up, because my father wasn't usually so effusive. "Aw, thank you, Dad," I managed to say. "I love you too." I hung up the phone with a heavy heart and I told myself something ludicrous: *Ashley, the attack happened. And you can't do anything about it. You need to tuck this away and forget it ever happened.*

Forget it ever happened? As if I ever could. Once again, I was employing my old coping mechanisms— *Buck up, little camper! You can get past this, too, if you just pray some surface prayers and get really, really plucky.* As if pluck ever cured anyone from soul damage.

Remember how we talked about stuffing unpleasant emotions in invisible boxes and telling anger, and other unpleasant emotions, to behave? Essentially, I was telling my trauma to behave. Be good. Toe the line. Mind your p's and q's. And keep out of mischief.

Unfortunately, trauma is very badly behaved and does not stay in any kind of box for long.

"Tuck this away…"? In the words of Dr. Phil, I would like to say to my twenty-two-year-old self, "How's that working out for you?"

And if she was being honest, my twenty-two-year-old self would answer, "Not well." Trauma is not, as I found out, tuckable.

For the next two years I did more stuffing than an assembly line worker at a teddy bear factory. *You can't do anything about it…Forget it ever happened.*

And I wrestled with God. Why had He allowed these things to happen? *I was practically perfect*, I thought. I didn't party. I didn't have sex. I lived a good, clean life to the best of my knowledge. So why me? Bitterness took root and began to grow like a weed.

I gained weight, and strangely, I didn't even care for the first time in my life. But not because I was healthy and whole. My spirit, along with my body, was heavier than ever. Part of it was that I was so angry at my attacker—and at men in general. I didn't want to look good for a man if that's what men were—brutal and unfeeling. I had always dreamed that someday I would have a really beautiful love story. I'd meet a man that would make me feel like my waiting had been worth it. But at this point in my life a love story was the very last thing I wanted. I hated the idea of opening up and trusting a man. I wanted to be left alone. If a guy even glanced at me with a twinkle in his eye, I would zap him with mental pepper spray.

I don't think so, Buster. Keep away!

My work was affected too. I remember being at a photo shoot and my then-agent glaring at me.

"I didn't know there was a *weight problem* here," she sniped. The two words "weight problem" were particularly acidic.

Nice. Yeesh, woman, what do you think this is— Skinny Days at Fat Camp? Your agency represents all different kinds of shaped girls! Figure girls! Curve girls!

Her sour comment stirred my resentment. I thought of some unholy words for her, the modeling industry, men in general, and if I'm being honest, humanity in general. My pluck was turning to prickles.

My work decreased by large amounts, not just because of my weight gain. I had only gained about ten pounds, so despite my agent's cutting comments this was not a deal breaker for most clients. My opportunities decreased because I didn't take hold of them. On more than one occasion I would be driving over to Miami to meet with a new potential client or a really great casting that promised to be lucrative. And halfway there I would stop and turn around. It was so difficult to watch everything I had been working so hard for begin to fall to pieces.

My feelings festered and grew unmanageable. I became depressed. The sadness and anger infiltrated every area of my life. I was living in the most beautiful, expensive condo and I would cry myself to sleep almost every night. Panic attacks became a normal occurrence. I woke up nearly every night for a year, seized with anxiety and fear. A fog followed me wherever I went, though I was still trying to conceal it.

My family began to notice the changes, though it was easier to hide from far away. My phone calls home were less frequent, and even when I did call them, the conversations were short and my answers even shorter. They were confused at my sharpness, which made me feel worse because I didn't want to be that way. I just didn't know how to snap back to my old, bubbly self again. I just wanted to make it through and be happy again. But my pain was leaking out, and the ones who loved me most were concerned.

Of course, my Father in Heaven was more concerned still. He knew better than anyone that I was bending, bending, *bending*, and soon I would break.

Bend toward Me, sweet girl! He whispered. *I'm*

*here! I am the source of healing your heart needs. Turn
back, My love. Come back to Me…*

Sadly, my path curved away from Him, not toward
Him. I started to walk on that path, and then I began
to run.

After one particular modeling trip, I knew I had hit
a personal low. I had just flown in from being paid
thousands of dollars to stay and work at a luxury re-
sort in Mexico. Tough life, right? People looked at my
fabulous existence on Facebook and saw all of my glit-
tery pictures of white sand and aquamarine ocean and
thought, *Look at Ashley go!*

But inside I was dying. While I never actually con-
templated suicide I prayed that God would just take
me. I didn't want to go on the way I was going. One
night I called my dad.

"Dad, I'm worried about myself. I am hurting so
bad and I truly don't think I can go on. I know I'm a
Christian but I don't see the point in my life right now.
I want God to take me."

I had just flown in from Mexico and was flying out
the next morning to another glamorous job. I was living a life most people only dream of, but I just wanted
to go to sleep and never wake up again.

For almost two years, I just existed. I was stuck in
quicksand, unable to heal from the past and powerless
to move forward. While I hadn't abandoned my faith,
I had deserted all but a surface practice of it. Yes, I believed that God was God and Jesus was Jesus. True,
when pressed, I would have told anyone that I was
a Christian. But beneath that top layer of basic creed
and worldview, I was as frozen as Lot's wife. A pillar
of salt. A decent facsimile of a good Christian girl.

Of course, our Father loves His girls way too much to let them get away with mere functioning. "I came that they may have life and have it abundantly," Jesus promises in John 10:10 (ESV). Do you believe it?

Sometimes, abundance is growing underground, silently and lavishly, ready to burst through the dead, rocky earth and surprise us with verdant, green new life.

When I look back, I see how God used three "seeds" to usher spring into my wintry existence. It took me two years, but I finally broke down and told my parents about the attack. I had no idea how powerful the secret had become, building up fearsome muscle as I stuffed it into the Don't Go There box. A secret like that is a little bit like one of those old and slightly disturbing jack-in-the-box toys. You wind the handle, over and over, knowing that creepy Jack is building up a head of steam. You hold your breath. You're unsettled, unnerved. It's always worse before it pops out, isn't it? And then that monstrous thing explodes and scares the life out of you. But at least you can breathe again. At least the dread is gone.

That's the way it was for me with my secret. I stuffed it, managed it, tried to control its power, but in the end I had to tell my loved ones. As awkward and difficult as that conversation was, the relief afterward was enormous. My parents were loving and supportive, and I felt a bit better for the first time in years. By exposing what had happened to me, suddenly there was more air, more light. And I began to slowly uncover my bruised soul to God's comforting hands.

We've all endured negative things. Sometimes, we even have untold damage that needs to be dealt with.

Have you ever swept some deep hurt under the rug, hoping it would just go away?

How'd that work out for you? (Dr. Phil again.)

If you're ready for emotional healing, know that your Father is right there, longing to help and heal. The first thing you need to do is face the truth. Maybe you're like I was, an expert at building walls and stuffing things into dark corners. Take it from me—you can't pretend forever.

It takes courage to face the things you have buried for so long. What will people think? We wonder, *What if I am rejected, misjudged, or unloved by those I care about? If so-and-so knew what happened to me, their good opinion will surely turn to a bad one, right?*

There's something about speaking the truth out loud to another person that does wonders. But make sure the person you choose is trustworthy. Pray and ask God to give you wisdom on who to share with and when to share it.

There's a saying I believe is true: "That which is denied is never healed."

Does that ring true for you?

Nobody can be healed until they're willing to say, "I've got a problem, and I need help with it."

The writer Nora Ephron said, "Be the heroine in your own life, never the victim." Ask God for wisdom. Whatever your problem may be, face it. If you don't, you run the risk of letting the problem grow and even take over your life, like I did for too long.

Our past experiences may have made us the way we are, but we don't have to stay that way. There's always an off-ramp toward a new, better direction.

When I think about my niece, Makenna, I think about how God used her to set in motion my turn for the better. Her coming to this world was the beginning of me coming back to life again. She was the beginning of my curving toward something good instead of warping into someone bent beyond recognition.

Before I found out she was on her way to us, I was spending so much energy wrestling with God. I was trying to block Him from my heart at the very time I needed His healing presence the most. I kept pushing my Father away, but the more I pushed, the more He was there, gentle but insistent. Beckoning me back to life, but not life as usual. He was inviting me to a new life, a richer existence than the one I had had prior to the attack.

He wastes nothing, you know. He has the ability to make all things new, even something as wretched as a physical attack.

I look back in astonishment. I was so stuck in my bitterness, so lost in my fog. I might have known He would rescue me. I might have known the One who came to earth as a baby would use a baby to light my way.

When I learned my older sister, Andrea, was pregnant with her first baby, I felt a spark of hope. My life had been difficult, bland, for a few years, and then all of a sudden there was promise. My mindset shifted from myself to this new life. I began to want to spend more time with my sister and by extension, my whole family. I didn't even know if the baby was a boy or a girl, but I secretly hoped for a girl.

When I found out my wish would come true, that a baby girl was coming to our family, I was excited.

When was the last time I had felt so positive about my life? The fog was lifting, and Andrea still had twenty weeks to go in her pregnancy.

Instantly—and I do mean in a *flicker*—I had a thought: *I want to teach this little one. I want to show her all the things I've had to learn the hard way.*

Suddenly, my murky reality was shot through with a ray of purpose. I wanted this little girl—so precious to me already—to know she was beautiful, to understand her worth in a way I never had as a young girl.

Obviously, it was fun to think about spoiling her with ridiculously cute outfits and doing her hair. Definitely, I was already angling for Best Aunt Ever. Yet the spark I felt was about much more than tiny tulip dresses and French braids. I wanted to be the person I wish I'd had to encourage me as I grew.

Have you ever seen this saying on a sign or a meme? "Be the person you needed when you were younger."

Who did *I* need when I was younger, coming up through the world so insecure, so bent in the direction of whatever or whoever would make me feel less alone?

I needed someone who would say, "Honey Child, you are already beautiful. You already have endless worth. Your story is this: God chose you and loves you. If you wander off, He will find you. If you are scared, He will calm your anxious heart. If you are broken, He will repair the secret, hidden cracks inside of you. If you are full of shame, He will cover you in delight. If you give up on Him, He will not give up on you."

I wanted to be there for her. I aspired to teach her, from the moment she could grasp it, that she is special, loved, and found in Christ. She would have more peace and confidence than I ever did, if she believed me. If she believed her Father. I wanted her brand-new life to be different.

When Makenna was born, I prayed truth over her life, even though I had been barely praying myself. I sang truth to her, about her fundamental value as God's creation, His girl, even though I had been struggling against God for so long. Something in me budged. My heart began to soften again. Almost like a bulb flower after a long winter. You know, one of those glorious, exuberant little flowers that take your breath away after a season of biting winds, gray skies, and frozen earth? A daffodil, a crocus, an iris. Just as the ground begins to warm and thaw, they emerge, earlier than any other flowers.

To me, it's interesting that those exquisite shapes and vivid colors are still flowers underneath that cold, hard winter ground. They can be beautiful again, it just takes the right conditions to coax them to bloom. I was still beautiful underneath the cold, hard winter. Around Makenna's birth, conditions started to change for me. Her birth was a development. A curve in the right direction. And another plot twist was coming around the corner.

I had not been regularly attending church for quite a while. I never deserted my faith, but in my own way I had pushed God out of the center of my life. I was trapped in my questions and anger, wondering if God truly cared about me.

Somehow Makenna's birth, and the accompanying hope I felt, drew me back to church—and faith. I had been stumbling down a road thick with uncertainty and then all of a sudden everything felt clearer, lighter. The blessing of Makenna helped point me back in the right direction.

For months after her birth, I would go to church and sit in the back, barely holding back the tears every single week. My heart was cautious and wary, comparable to a rescue dog who came from something bad and can't quite trust the love of her adoptive parents.

I was kind of like one of those rescue dogs. I knew that I had been rescued and saved, but I wasn't sure I really wanted to allow God back into my life, at least not fully. I was still defensive and hurting. I was still pulling away. But I wanted and craved to be back in His arms, enfolded in His love. I pined to be set free.

Sunday after Sunday, I sat alone, feeling the tug at my heart grow stronger. One particular Sunday morning, though, was different. God was about to win our marathon wrestling match.

The night before, I had a dream about the pastor of my church. It was one of those intense, you-are-there, crazy-real dreams that startle you so much you wake up instantly. In the dream, the pastor was preaching: "What are you holding on to?" he said. "What is it going to take for you to let go?"

I thought this was an odd little clip of a dream. I drifted back to sleep wondering at how tangible it seemed.

The next day I went to church as had become my new habit. That morning, I was feeling more like myself. I knew my love for God was real. I had been praying more and more, about anything and everything. But I hadn't taken a crucial step. I hadn't asked my Father to help me move past all that had happened and uproot the bitterness that had been choking me.

I leaned in and listened attentively as the pastor preached about Jacob and how he wrestled with the Angel of the Lord. Jacob refused to let go until the Angel blessed him. Sure, ever after the patriarch walked with a limp, but *he knew God better*. We grow in relationship with the Lord when we bring Him our questions, doubts, and fears and wrestle with Him.

I had never thought of it that way. I had been pushing God away, but God is not set aside easily. While I persisted in pushing, God refused to go away and kept on pulling me back to Him.

After finishing reading Jacob's story in Scripture, the pastor asked if some of us might be in a place where we were wrestling with God. Struggling. Pushing. Pulling.

"What are you holding on to?" he said. "What is it going to take for you to let go?"

Down to his emphasis on certain syllables, the pastor's words were the same as in my dream.

My jaw was on the floor. I could hardly believe my ears. God had spoken to me in a dream. He had a message specifically for me, but was I ready to listen? Although I had never been the kind of person to spring from my chair and rush forward for prayer after a church service, I did just that as soon as the pastor gave the all-clear (er, the benediction).

I asked God to release me from all that had been holding me back from experiencing a full relationship with Him: *Father, forgive me for allowing myself to become so angry and bitter and blaming those around me, for blaming You.* As I prayed, tears spilled down my cheeks. *Give me a new beginning with You, Jesus. Here and now I am letting go. No more wrestling. And like Jacob, Lord, would You also bless me?*

Remember the three seeds I said God had planted in me to help me emerge from my "bleak midwinter"?

1. I finally told my parents and family members about my attack, disempowering my secret and exposing it to air, light, and healing.
2. My niece, Makenna, was born, ushering in a new purpose for me: to be the person for her I wish I'd had when I was growing up.
3. God spoke to me in a dream, asking me, "What are you holding on to? What is it going to take for you to let go?" And I dropped the rope, so to speak. The tug of war was over as I stopped pulling away and submitted everything to Him—including my past.

Having properly dealt with it, my past was where it belonged. Spring had sprung, and everything felt new. New mindset. New heart. New path. And then, just because He is a generous Father, He planted one more "seed" to show me the way.

I had flown to Dallas to do some modeling work for JC Penney through a connecting flight in Charlotte. After spending about three days in Dallas, I flew back through the same connecting flight back to Charlotte. When I took my seat on the flight back, I sat next to a man who works and travels with Josh McDowell, a well-known Christian apologist, author, and speaker.

"Pete" told me that he recognized me from the

flight out to Dallas three days earlier. He was traveling with Josh and their team for an apologetics conference the same days I worked the JC Penney job. Now here we were again by chance on the same flight back. After our three-hour conversation, though, I knew there had been nothing random about it. God had orchestrated for me and Pete to sit next to each other—no doubt about it.

As we talked, Pete and I didn't even notice the hours. When the flight attendants would ask us if we wanted peanuts or cookies, we were both startled. *What? Why would you interrupt such an intense dialogue for trivialities?* Ha! (Flight attendant was all, "Hey, I'm *supposed* to ask!")

Pete was a stranger to me when we got on that airplane, but I trusted him immediately and did not hold back much as I answered his questions about my life, family, and our shared beliefs. Very carefully, I told him about the attack. Pete was a true spiritual brother to me in that moment. He encouraged me to share my story with others in the context of my faith someday "when the time is right."

Wow—that blew my mind. I had never considered such a thing, but maybe, just maybe, Pete was right. Maybe God could use me and my story for His glory. It would be a while before I did share my story, but my conversation with Pete was a big part of God preparing my heart to serve Him in a new way.

It was time to move on. God had been clear: "Ashley, you've been in a difficult season. I am asking you to leave that behind after a time of wrestling with Me. Trust Me. Move forward. You may walk with a limp but you cannot stay here and continue wrestling. I have much more for you."

So I moved forward in faith. I never experienced another panic attack or cried myself to sleep again. I stopped waking up in the middle of the night with unexplainable fear. Things were clearly different.

I had come to know the Lord at a very early age, but until then I didn't know much about God's tangible work in a believer's life. I didn't know how real and true the words of Scripture are when they tell us, "Behold, He is making all things new" (see Revelation 21:5).

God was real to me as never before and my love for Him increased.

I began to dream again.

It's amazing what happens when you leave junk behind. It's easier to be you—to be who you already are. I started to consistently give my life over to God on a daily basis. I pressed in to my relationship with my Father, knowing life would always throw me curves but that He would show me the way forward.

Slowly, surely, my life began to transform. I stopped trying to be anything but myself. I know, right? What a concept! Me being me. My modeling career was still going but I stopped trying to be thin enough or pretty enough for that career. I didn't worry about my body like I had in the past. I simply tried to live in balance, checking in constantly with the One who created balance and generated joy. I waited to see what God would bring my way. A career change? Maybe. A husband? Maybe. A reality show? Maybe.

Wait—what?

I still can't believe what happened next.

After a family Christmas in Michigan that year, I

flew back to Florida after watching the entire world, or so it seemed, with their relationships, engagements, weddings, and babies as I flew solo. In the past this single lady status would have done me in. And we all know Christmas singleness is the worst (well, next to Valentine's singleness)! But overall, I was still content. Content, but wondering what was next for me.

I had a serious conversation with my dad over the phone.

"Dad, my life has been good but extremely silent the last year, quiet, uneventful," I said. "I'm happy. I've been growing so much in my walk with the Lord. But I need a major shake-up. I want this year to be a life-changing one. I need to get married or have a career change or *soooomething*!"

He said he would pray for me and we hung up. That night while I was asleep I got an email from a casting agent asking me to be a part of something new. There was a reality dating show in the works called *Coupled*. They wanted more racial and body diversity than *The Bachelor* franchise. Body diversity? Boy, did I ever have some body diversity! It clicked—once again, my curves, my size, were the very reason I was being sought out.

They wondered, would I be interested in meeting with them to see what the possibilities might be?

"Um, no. No thanks! I would never in a million years do something like that," I said. At first.

I prayed about it, although it seemed ridiculous to do so. But something in me stirred. The more I learned about the show, the more intrigued I became.

But, but...good Christian girls don't go on reality dating shows...I sputtered.

God's answer was all kinds of crazy. *Oh, but you aren't a good Christian girl, you're so much more than that. You are beautiful to me, and I want to take you on a world-enlarging adventure.*

Against the odds, God seemed to be saying, "Go in this direction, daughter of Mine. This is what I have for you next."

It was a development. A plot twist. And as I was to find out, this show was indeed a curve in the right direction.

Beauty Box

1. Have you ever blamed yourself for something you did nothing to deserve?

2. Have you ever zapped anyone, or a whole group of people—say, men—with "mental pepper spray"? What were the circumstances? Did it make you feel better or worse?

3. "I came that they may have life and have it abundantly," Jesus promises in John 10:10 (ESV). Do you believe it? Some translations use the word "fullness" instead of abundance. On a scale of one to ten, how much fullness are you experiencing right now? Pray and ask your Father for wisdom to discern the first steps in a life of fullness.

4. Have you ever swept some deep hurt under the rug, hoping it would just go away?

5. How'd that work out for you?

6. Was there ever a season in your life where you felt as though you were wrestling with God? Say it with me: "When life throws you curves, bend toward Him, not away from Him."

7. What does Nora Ephron's saying, "Be the heroine in your own life, never the victim," mean to you?

8. "Be the person you needed when you were younger." Who did *you* need when you were younger?

9. Has God ever spoken to you in a dream? Were you ready to listen?

10
REALITY

I laughed, actually. Out loud. When I read that email from the *Coupled* casting director. The whole thing seemed cuckoo for Cocoa Puffs. It was truly chuckle-worthy. Me? Be on some show where I'd have to flounce around in a bathing suit, clawing my way to the front of a pack of beauties, before a live television audience—all to snag a man?

This girl does not sit in hot tubs with strange—albeit cute—men. Never mind on TV!

This girl does not stand around, waiting with bated breath to find out if she will or will not be extended the offer of a rose!

"Hello, earth to producers! I will never find my Christian husband on a secular reality dating show!"

I thought you wanted a shake-up in your safe, comfortable life? God said, kindly speaking to me in the secret places of my heart.

You can't seriously be for *this, Lord,* I sputtered. *I mean, have You seen* Bachelor in Paradise?

Yet I felt an undeniable nudge to explore this thing further. His hand was gently, surely guiding me along. And the more I learned, the more I opened to the possibility.

The casting agent explained to me that *Coupled* was

a new kind of reality dating show, more open to people of faith. No roses either. The setup was completely different.

She encouraged me to go for it, that my strong morals would be an asset, not a drawback, for this show. The executive producer was none other than reality TV mogul Mark Burnett of *Survivor* and *The Voice* fame. Burnett and his wife, Roma Downey, are outspoken Christians. He wanted this dating show to have a strong emphasis on compatibility rather than hookups.

I liked what I was hearing about the show, but I was still pretty much petrified. What in the world could I be thinking?

Next thing you know, I was flown out to LA to meet with a room full of producers who asked me about three hundred thousand questions. One of the questions asked was, "What's important to you in your sex life?" My answer: "I don't have a sex life!" *This* got their attention. There were also questions on my views on dating, sex, and marriage. What kind of man was I looking for?

Later, after the personality tests, when I was being grilled by the producers, sex came up again.

When I uttered the words, "I'm a virgin," I thought we had all been swallowed up by a giant cone of silence. Had there been crickets in the room, they would have chirped. Loudly. The producers might have been less surprised if I had said, "I'm here to do espionage for the Russians." They were floored.

One of the producers asked me a pointed question: "What happens if you fall deeply in love with someone, and the guy wants to sleep with you? What if (not sleeping with him) was the deal breaker at that point?"

Fair question, and the answer was simple: "Then he's not the guy for me," I said. "Obviously, it would be incredibly painful if I had strong feelings for him, but again, I would know he wasn't right for me."

Well, that's that. No way will they want someone like me on their show. Let's face it, they probably think I am a giant freak. I'm okay with that. I stood up for what I believed in, so there! Job well done!

I also thought, *I will never hear from them again in this lifetime or the next.*

A month later I was on my way to Anguilla to start filming *Coupled*, asking myself if I had lost my ever-loving mind.

It all seemed so crazy, scary, and completely out of my comfort zone, but at the same time I had felt the okay from God to go forward. Be careful what you pray for, ladies! I had asked my Father to shake up my safe, predictable world and He had done exactly that.

When I stepped off the airplane in Anguilla I felt like I was having an out-of-body experience. I didn't really know what I was doing or why I was doing it, but I had been propelled along on a totally random, kind of scary, and completely out-of-norm opportunity.

The tropical heat washed over me in waves, adding to my feeling of unreality. My head was spinning. The air smelled like tropical flowers and fruits, and palm trees swayed overhead, filtering the bluest of skies.

Everyone in my life will think I am nuts. They will also consider me a little less spiritual. Less of a good Christian girl. But somehow, that didn't bother me nearly as much as it would have in the past. I was confident God had given me the green light, whether or not this endeavor seemed "spiritual." I was secure in the knowledge that He would get me through. I alone knew how much time I had spent in prayer before going forward.

I had come a long way in my body image issues, but...true confession, I wondered how I would look on TV. The camera adds ten pounds at least, and I would be the one average-size girl among a group of size 2s. *You'll look so big next to all of them...* my insecurities rustled and hissed. *Maybe millions of people will see your flaws up close...*

Hey—you! It was time for a holy self-talk pep rally.

You were chosen for this show because of your size— your very relatable size! And more important, your Father wants you to be here for some beautiful purpose that right now only He knows. Trust Him! He will not let you down.

So shut up, Satan! Hush, insecurities! Step into your God-given confidence and shake the dust off your self-loathing past. Keep walking. March out of your comfort zone, girl (hup, hup!). Yes, being filmed 24/7 as the "big" girl among a bevy of small, gorgeous ladies will challenge you, but depend on it, God is beside you, in front of you, and behind you on this journey. You are hemmed in, baby. Zipped up in love and worth! Stay close to the Father and you will emerge from this experience stronger and more confident than before.

I was growing, but human. My poise was to be tested over and over while I taped the show. I read an article about the show, focused on me, from the *Huffington Post*. They featured a big picture of me taken from the most unflattering angle (obviously selected for just that), in a swimsuit and towel. The article discussed my weight, my "level" of prettiness, and the fact that I was a curve model on a reality dating show. The tone was critical, not just of me but of the other girls on the show.

But somehow I was able to let it go pretty quickly, knowing that things like this would happen. After all, I was the first plus model to go a full season on a reality dating show. I was different and I would draw attention, both positive and negative.

The premise of the show was also different from anything viewers had ever seen in terms of reality TV dating. Twelve women, including me, were flown to Anguilla, a breathtakingly beautiful island in the Caribbean and…wait—Anguilla? Yeah, things got "unreal" pretty quickly on this reality show.

There we were, twelve single girls, on a "quest for love," according to the press releases. The cast included Miss Arizona USA 2009, Alicia-Monique Blanco; Miss Colorado USA 2015, Talyah Polee; and "Theme Park Princess" TT Baker. (TT looked so much like Tiana from *The Princess and the Frog*, I was always half expecting her to break into song, twirl, or kiss an animated frog!)

Each week different men would come to Anguilla and meet each of us briefly in a speed dating–like one-on-one. After meeting, we had the choice to go right—saying yes to pursuing the man some more—and join him at the tiki bar. We could also choose to go left—saying no to spending any more time with him—and go back to the bungalow to wait for the next contestant. Sound familiar? The left/right process was inspired by the dating app Tinder, in which you swipe left or right depending on if you are feeling a spark or not.

It was irresistible to guess who would "swipe" right or left based on discernible chemistry or lack thereof. Sometimes it was easy to guess, but other times there were surprises.

If you did swipe right, you were not alone at the tiki bar with the guy. Oh, no! Every girl who also walked right would be there, each one vying for their chance to somehow stand out in the eyes of that week's contestant. It became a contest from that moment on. Of course, at this stage everyone was still on their best behavior. No one wanted to look pushy or desperate.

You know, just sitting here in a tiki bar on national TV, flipping my hair and pretending I don't care if I am chosen or not. Act natural!

Awkward? Yes, hopelessly. At least, I felt hopelessly awkward in my two forays to the tiki bar, but more on that later.

Back to the premise of the show: The women who chose to go to the tiki bar awaited the guy, and when he showed up, they would spend a few more minutes together in a group setting, ostensibly to give the contestant one more chance to read the room. From this group, the man would then choose two ladies with whom he would like to forge a deeper bond. And then it was off to the spectacular villas, where the man would spend one-on-one time with each girl to gain a sense of their connection—or disconnection.

The parallel in real life would be...wait a minute...there is no real-life equivalent! There is no situation in which a guy asks two girls out at the same time (two girls sitting next to each other), takes them to the same locale for a date, parks one girl for hours at a time while he gets to know the other girl, and then chooses which one he will continue to date! Yet that was the setup, and it made for pretty good TV. Meanwhile, Amish bundling and Zulu courting huts would have been more based in reality than this bizarre dating model.

After the guy had chosen which of two girls to become "coupled" with, the chosen girl stayed at the villa with him (and other coupled pairs) to explore a possible relationship, and the other girl would return to the bungalows to await the next contestant.

Got it? That was *Coupled*. If you were paired up with someone, you would end up spending up to six weeks getting to know them at the villas. At the end of their stay, the couples would be faced with the decision to continue their relationship back in the United States or to end it. Of course, season finales being what they are, this wasn't just a simple conversation.

"Hey, it's been a slice! But you know what, this isn't working for me so let's just cherish the memories and move on—apart."

No, it was much more dramatic. Each man and each woman in the couple had to decide separately whether or not they wanted to continue the relationship. If, say, the woman decided yes, she would wait at a helicopter pad in fraught anticipation to see if her man would join her there. You know, the old "wait at the helipad for me. If I don't show, it means we are breaking up" routine. In real life, one might have gotten a text in the parking lot of Jiffy Lube: "I'm just not that into you." But on *Coupled*, it was the helipad.

If the setup for the ending seemed dramatic when

it was explained to me, that was nothing compared to what actually happened. There was melodrama galore, my friends, and somehow my "match" and I were at the center of it.

Going in, I had decided that in order for a relationship to work out on this show, two things would have to happen:

1. The man would have to have a genuine faith.
2. He would have to bring his faith up first, before me, so I would know it wasn't just a ploy to date me.

Enter B.T., the third bachelor contestant with whom we were presented. From the moment we met, I felt drawn to him, although I didn't find out anything about his faith in our initial one-on-one meeting. He was a thirty-year-old ex-soldier who now made a great living modeling for the covers of romance novels. He was extremely fit, with the kind of build you might imagine on someone depicted on the front of a bodice ripper. *Mamma Mia!* He was crazy attractive. He was also sweet, and solid, somehow. There was a gravity to him that set him apart. Maybe it was the fact that he had been through so much in life already. He had served our country proudly and even though he had lost part of his leg in war, he held a passion for life that you don't often find. One of my favorite attributes was that he had a servant's heart. I would often wonder where he was while filming with the group only to find him helping clean up the kitchen so the staff could get home to their own kids. I had immense respect for that man when it came to that.

Interestingly, B.T. and I had modeling in common, but we also had both struggled with body image, me with my lifelong dissatisfaction with being built a certain way, and him trying to come to terms with the piece of his body that had been stolen from him and would never be restored. I sensed a connection and decided to go right.

It was my second foray into the tiki bar. The first time I didn't know what I was doing, literally, and going right just seemed like the thing to do. However, the first guy, Tyler, did not choose me, which was for the best. The second guy was nice, but I didn't feel a special link to him so I turned left.

Quite a few girls had swiped right for B.T. The tiki bar was buzzing with anticipation when he arrived. One of the girls asked him what he was looking for in a partner.

"I am looking for someone who can help me grow spiritually," he said, adding, "I attend a non-denominational church and that's important to me."

Note to self: Shut mouth. Don't gape—you're on television! But *Yowza!* B.T. seemed to have a genuine faith. Check! And he brought it up without knowing anything about me. Check, check!

On my end, the deal was sealed. *That's the person you are going to date while being here*, I thought. But would I be one of his choices?

B.T. ended up choosing me and Kristin, a gorgeous fireball of a girl who had traveled the world and started her own business. Kristin was an absolute sweetheart, but it was hard not to feel dull and irrelevant around her. We—the three of us—strapped on our life jackets and zipped to the villas in a gleaming red speedboat. Upon arrival, B.T., Kristin, and I had what was probably the world's most awkward "date."

Yes, there were three of us on that date, and the whole setup did not play to my strengths. I am not a girl who chases or fights for attention in a group setting. Of course, that's the whole point of the tiki bar and the villa dates: *See me! Notice me! Pick me!*

I was absolutely drained during my dinner out with B.T. and Kristin. It had been a long day and I couldn't keep up as she regaled us with adventurous stories of traveling alone in the Himalayas or whatever dangerous, dark mountain ranges she had conquered in her exotic lifetime. Kristin seemed unattainably perfect, so naturally sexy and confident to the max. And I was not. I felt self-conscious and uncomfortable, especially with cameras in our faces. My eyes were literally drooping as I fought sleepiness. Wouldn't that have made for tantalizing TV? If my unconscious face had dropped into my plate of mahimahi?

I shudder just to think of it. I could not wrap my mind around the fact that after our date, I had to go share a big ole California king-size bed with this girl after we finished "competing" for the same guy! And there would be cameras filming us as we slept!

(Yes, the cameras were on, even when I slept, which took some getting used to. Even after I got back home after the show had taped, it took me a few months to feel completely comfortable when I slept! Everyone else in the cast said the same thing about their post-show experience.)

It was just too much for one little brain to handle. Still, I found myself hoping B.T. would pick me but was sure he would not. Why would he? It was like

B.T. had a choice between a blonde Snow White and Sleepy the Tall Dwarf!

When we were able to have some one-on-one time the next day, I knew I had to tell B.T. about my faith and my values on the topic of sex. I would not only be sharing this deeply personal part of me with B.T., but also millions of viewers. *Gasp.*

Would I be ridiculed by viewers? I thought it was a real possibility, but felt it was important. God had given me a platform to share Him and the countercultural life He had led me on. This was part of it, and I didn't want to back down. Also, in "real life" this topic would have come up just as quickly. Maybe not on the first date, but definitely on the second or third.

Ever since sex was on my radar as a young teen, I felt like God had called me to really trust Him specifically on this issue. I knew Scripture was clear that sex within marriage was God's best for His children, but I didn't really understand the exact reasons He wanted that for us, for me. But I wanted God to know my love for Him trumped any feelings, emotions, or desires regarding sex.

It hasn't always been easy. I have had so many questions along the way. I've seen many of my Christian friends make the choice to have sex outside of marriage, and it didn't seem to affect their relationship with their significant others or their relationship with God.

Well, look at her… Look at him. Maybe it's not that big of a deal after all…

But when I would listen to that Voice inside, I heard something else entirely! *No, Ashley. I have called you to this. I want you to follow Me and trust Me on this.*

Sex is a loaded topic, to put it mildly. It can trigger all sorts of different feelings and responses.

What are you thinking right now, sweet friend? What kinds of choices have you made in regard to sex?

I want you to know that I am not here to judge you. At all. I don't think any less of you. Only your loving, compassionate Father knows what you have been through in your life, and why you made the choices you made.

Your value in Him is unchanged, regardless of your past choices. Do you believe it?

Actually, that's the key. What *do* you believe? Do you believe in your God-breathed value to the point that it shapes your choices? Do you understand the reality of who you are? Loved. Cherished. A pearl of inestimable price. The Maker's costly work. Beautiful!

When we absorb that truth long enough, we start to believe it, and that belief influences our every thought and action.

By the time I found myself on *Coupled*, my identity had gone through an extensive makeover. I no longer thought of myself as chubby, unseen Ashley who had to try and prove herself worthy. I believed I was handcrafted, noticed every second of my life by a wise, all-knowing, ever-loving Father. He would see me through every step of this wild and weird journey into "reality." He would use an unreal situation in my life to show me what was real.

By the end of that first full day at the villa, B.T. was going to make his decision—me or Kristin. I was running out of time. With guts churning and prayers swirling, I sat him down to have the "talk." Hopefully, I would not pass out. With a full camera crew capturing my every halting word, I finally spit it out.

"Uh, I need to say this before we go any further...I am saving myself for marriage."

B.T. took in my news calmly. "I respect that, Ashley," he said gently. My stomach flipped. Well, that was over with! And he didn't laugh or freak out. Still, I was sure I'd be sent packing back to the bungalows that night.

So it was shocking when the host, Terrance B, brought me, B.T., and Kristin back together for the announcement. "I pick Ashley," B.T. said.

What??? Me??? This was insane. I was stunned and thrilled and panicky all at the same time. People, this reality was getting real.

The next month had me strapped into a roller coaster of high highs and low lows. The only way I got through it was knowing God was with me and sensing He was in me, my ever-present help.

One day we were filming on a boat and snorkeling. I didn't want to be there at all, never mind in a swimsuit. As I jumped into the water, I wanted to kick the camera man in the face with my flippers. Suddenly, it all felt so much more invasive and strange than I had ever imagined.

God! I'm not happy right now! What am I doing here?! Help!

My fractious feelings didn't go away immediately, but as we sailed back to the villas, my brain calmed. I could see this was all so fake in comparison to the real world, but God had led me here. He would hold me. He had an elite purpose for me, here, now, in a swimsuit, sitting next to a size 0 beauty queen. There was beauty in the peace that washed over me.

God was close to me—I felt it. One day soon after I arrived at the villas, I was emotionally exhausted and questioning everything. *Should I be here? What is the purpose for this? Did I make a mistake in coming to Anguilla?*

We had tons of downtime to do whatever, as long as we didn't mind cameras trailing along with us. I decided to pass on breakfast and go down to the beach alone. Well, alone until four camera crew people came hauling down the beach to find me. I just wanted to cry by myself! That was the most frustrating thing—the aggressive and constant invasion of privacy.

I just wanted to sit and think. Things with B.T. and me were up—and then they were down. It was all so confusing. One of my favorite producers found me as I sat on a huge rock by the ocean, a vulnerable puddle of a girl, surrounded by oodles of these tiny little crabs.

"I feel so insecure right now," I said through teary eyes. The crew felt for me—I could tell—but they had a job to do and the cameras kept rolling. They seemed to sense that I needed to be alone, so they headed back while I stayed, staring at the water and praying. It was such a strange situation, but in that moment I experienced God's devoted presence. I didn't know what my life would look like in a month, a year, forever, but I knew God held me there on that beach. My tears dried as I walked back to the villas, my heart lighter and more trusting than when I had left.

Dating can be so complicated, even in the real world away from cameras. Can I get an "Amen"? You put yourself out there, hoping to find your life's partner, and often you end up heartbroken, rejected, or otherwise emotionally wrung out. It can be more stressful than blissful. You worry, *Did he see the massive chunk of kale protruding from my teeth? Did he notice how inane my comment about current events was?* You wonder, *Will he call me again?* Sometimes, you hope he doesn't. Sometimes, you block him on your phone. Sigh.

I've mentioned before that I have always been intentional when it comes to dating. I don't want to go out for coffee with any old fella, just so I don't have to spend the evening in with Netflix and a gourmet assortment of chips and dip (although, that does sound good, come to think of it). And it's not like I am beating guys off with a stick. But if I *do* get asked out, I only want to go if the man has real potential to be my husband one day. And that is getting harder and harder as I get older.

I *have* tried online dating. So far it has not worked for this girl! Yes, I know. Your cousin Sally finally worked up the nerve to try an online dating website with "Mingle," "Harmony," or "Match" in the URL, and lo and behold! She found her soul mate, married him in a wedding covered by theknot.com (who did a lavish pictorial), and now they are expecting triplets!

I am happy for Sally, I truly am. But for me, online dating has been a frustrating waste of time so far. I am not opposed to trying it in the future, or to anyone else trying it in the future, but I think there should be some ground rules in place, don't you?

- Know who you are (it all comes back to identity, doesn't it?).

- Know how you want to be treated.
- Prayerfully consider what you are doing every step of the way.

Really, if those three guidelines are met, we can't go wrong. Whether it's meeting a guy online, on a blind date orchestrated by your best friend, or on a reality dating show, it's crucial to believe your worth, to trust that your value in God's eyes means you deserve to be treated accordingly, and to constantly pray for wisdom about your relationship.

Thankfully, by the time I was dating B.T., I was pretty solidly following my three-part "romance rubric" above.

I can honestly say I had an amazing time getting to know B.T. We had meaningful conversations about hardships we had faced, and spiritual goals we had set for ourselves.

We slept in separate rooms, though after he had chosen me at the villa, there was a sign on my bedroom doorplate that said "Ashley and B.T." *Uh, I don't think so.* B.T. had been immediately supportive when I asked for my own room.

When we got up in the morning, we would cook breakfast together. It was very sweet and cozy and companionable. I was starting to fall for him, and he for me. But in the end, as I prayerfully considered our relationship, I knew B.T. and I were not on the same page. Our faith meant different things to us. For me, faith was life. Something I would die for. Something I couldn't live without. I can't speak for him, but I always had the feeling we were in two different places on the journey.

I broke things off before we could even get to the helipad, and my decision was built up as one of the blockbuster stories on the season finale. We had only been together a month, but unlike real life where you might go on one or two dates per week, we had been together nearly every waking moment. Anytime you have that kind of heart connection, it's going to hurt when it's over. I cared intensely for B.T.; my feelings and tears were legit.

But I learned a crucial lesson on that show: I wanted a man who was just as passionate about loving the Lord with all his heart, soul, strength, and mind as I was. I still want someone who genuinely, wholeheartedly loves God, someone with a kind heart who puts others first.

Beyond passion for Jesus and basic kindness, I don't care if that man is a businessman, construction worker, musician, or teacher. Well, we do have to have some *zing, zang, zoom*! God made chemistry, and you can't fall in love without it. I hope that someone wonderful might be at the end of a church aisle someday, waiting for me. I hope that he appears someday soon! In the meantime, I am leaning into my Father's strong arms. He is building my faith as I live into the reality He has for me right now. *You are beautiful. Now. Without a man.*

Do you believe that?

"You complete me," Tom Cruise told Renée Zellweger in *Jerry Maguire*. I know. I swooned too. But when you think about it, that's a load of garbage. No human man can complete you. Only God can fulfill you and accomplish wholeness in your most hidden spaces. Only the Father can complete you.

I want to encourage those of you who are alone right now. By alone I mean "man-less." Sister, I get it. Flying solo in what feels like the Kingdom of Coupledom can just suck the scum at the bottom of the pond. Talk to God about it right this minute. Tell Him all your feelings of sadness and loneliness and rejection. He knows already, but telling Him is so important. Telling Him is a prayer for healing and hope. Listen closely as He will respond with love. He will infuse you with a calm and wholeness the world cannot understand.

And for you girls who are dating great guys? Handsome guys. Funny guys. Adorable guys. If they do not love the Lord like you do, it's time to move your sweet little booty far, far away.

"But, but, but…"

(I can hear you sputtering from here.)

I know. He leaves you Dunkin' Donuts iced coffee in the morning with the sweetest notes. Believe me, I adore iced coffee. But no. He's not the guy.

If you're picturing that scrawny theologian from your Grandma's church right now, the one with the allergies and the little Bible in his shirt pocket? Don't worry. He's not the guy either.

God's guy for you won't be like your mother's Brussels sprouts—you don't have to marry him because he's good for you but otherwise thoroughly unappealing.

God's guy for you will be appealing *and* good for you.

One of the hardest things ever is to walk away from a man who has your heart. But if you walk toward your Father, you will find something better, deeper, richer. Prince Charming himself could never touch the places inside you where Love already lives. Trust Him in this. Believe that your worth is found only and exclusively in God.

The reality is this: You are unfathomably beautiful, with or without a man. Are you starting to finally believe it?

Beauty Box

1. What's your favorite reality show to watch and why? Would you ever consider being on one? Which one?

2. For me, being on *Coupled* "seemed…completely out of my comfort zone." Have you ever sensed God was leading you way outside your comfort zone?

3. What did you think of my "holy self-talk pep rally"? Do you need to give yourself a holy self-talk pep talk?

4. Breakups on reality TV are dramatic. What was your most dramatic breakup? How did you deal with the aftermath?

5. When I had to go on a "trio date" with B.T. and Kristin, I said, "The whole setup did not play to my strengths." When was the last time you were in an overwhelming situation, which did not play to your strengths? How did you handle it?

6. Have you ever tried online dating? How did it work for you?

7. What do you think about my three-point "romance rubric"?

8. How much do you think you've bought into our culture's message that a man will complete you? What's one step you can take today to take hold of the truth—that only God can complete you?

11
CONFIDENT

To me, makeovers are irresistible. I'm a sucker for before and after shots, aren't you? There's something so pleasing about seeing pre- and post-makeover photos compared side by side.

Whether it's Emma Stone or someone's granny getting ambushed on the *Today* show, there's a wow factor about witnessing what hair and makeup tweaks can do for someone's glow. A few well-placed caramel highlights and a layered, razor cut take someone's look from stodgy to striking. Of course, no makeover is complete without a fantastic face to go with a great new hairstyle. The makeup artist will work his magic, smudging soft violet shadow on the woman's lids, adding depth to her blue/green eyes. A sweep of mascara, a shimmer of pink blush, and a swipe of matte berry lip color completes the beauty renovation, and the lucky woman is altered, made over.

One of the best parts is how that woman positively radiates a new confidence after her transformation. There's been a change, a revolution in how she feels as well as how she looks!

As you've read through this book, you've been privy to the stages of my "model makeover." Hopefully, as you walked with me, you underwent your own emotional and spiritual transformation. My heart's desire is for you to experience a revolution of your own, understanding in a new way what it means to be confident in the Father, assured of your God-infused identity.

The very concept of "confident" means so much more to me now.

I had spent most of my twenty-eight years feeling unseen, not good enough to be noticed by others as more than a blip on their radars. Today I know God is always present, reassuring me, covering my pain and yours in the shadow of His wings. We are never invisible to Him.

You are worth noticing, and loved tenderly.

Confidence understands that God wastes nothing, including the inevitable pain of rejection we will feel in this sin-damaged world. It's standing on the bedrock knowledge that when you feel overlooked, you can deepen your relationship with Someone who chooses you every time.

You are handpicked, exceptional, and distinctive to Him.

The world will always beat you down—or try to. You will never be pretty "enough" or thin "enough" to meet our culture's impossible standards.

But God's holy daughters have a sureness that overrides the media's confusing messages. When we saturate our minds with God's love and care, we embrace balance and strength. We know, on a level far beneath the white noise of our society that, pretty or not, He comes for us anyway.

You are captivating and adorable, just the way you are.

The more time we spend with God, the more we are convinced. There is no way that you or I could ever become more valuable to Him than we are at this very moment.

True confidence fights the twisted idea that one's worth is dependent on a dress size. Filled with assurance, we begin to care more about how our bodies *feel* rather than *look*.

We have a Father who is waiting for us to unload all that heavy, *heavy* body negativity onto His omnipotent shoulders.

You were made for unlimited goodness, not severe restriction. *You* were made for order, not disorder. *You* were made to treat your body with honor, dignity, and so much grace.

Real confidence also rejects the false salvation of chasing an impossible standard of beauty. What is *beautiful*? God's definition is worlds apart (literally) from our planet's shallow, small characterization. Confident women believe God when He says, "*You* are beautiful, My darling, the apple of My eye."

We also believe with certainty that we each have a rightful place at our Father's banqueting table. Instead of scratching for the grubs of this world—chicken-like—we are sure we belong to the sky.

Like Queen Esther, we know that God has set a royal crown on our heads, that only He confers a profound sense of meaning in our lives.

You were pursued by a King for a specific and elite purpose.

Genuine confidence also has a certain coolness to it. "Cool" says no striving. No pretending. No performing. It says, "You know what? I'm not enough, but that's okay, because Jesus is." It counteracts the frantic nature of perfectionism with healthy habits. God's coolness is deep calling to deep, authenticity calling for an authentic response. *Relax. Breathe. Be.*

You are God's workmanship, already perfect, holy, kept, and loved.

Sometimes, our newfound composure is tested. Life in this broken world means we will have terrible days. We will suffer.

And when we do, dignity digs deep for the answers. It wrestles with what has gone wrong. It grapples with God. But yet, there is something unshakeable at the bottom of our troubles—an immovable Rock.

When we experience painful losses and injustices, we feel anything but beautiful. Even so, dignity insists, "I know that my Redeemer lives" (Job 19:25 ESV).

God says, "You've been in a difficult season. I am asking you to leave that behind after a time of wrestling with Me. Trust Me. Move forward. You may walk with a limp but you cannot stay here and continue wrestling. I have much more for you."

You are made even more beautiful by your suffering.

From time to time, the path to true wholeness, peace, and body acceptance hits a curve in the road. A grace-full response is to bend with the curve, and allow our Father to take us in a direction we've never been before.

You are beautiful to me, and I want to take you on a world-enlarging adventure.

Finally, being confident in Christ means that you believe in your God-breathed value. You understand the reality of who you are: treasured, delightful, and worth it. This understanding influences what kinds of relationships you will pursue and how you should be treated. If the God of the universe cherishes you, shouldn't a mere mortal man do the same?

You are lovable, with or without a man.

Confidence, as God defines it, is more of everything good.

More grace.

More strength.

More boldness.

More freedom.

More.

When you are made over by God, the transformation is dramatic (but wearable). He revamps your "hidden person of the heart" without making you unrecognizable (1 Pet. 3:4 ESV). He restores you to the woman you are already—His image bearer. *So lovely.*

Dear friend, we've come to the end of our restoration journey together. I've loved every minute of it. By all means, feel free to steal any of these makeover secrets and make them your own. Share with those you love.

And remember always,

You are beautiful.

Believe it!

ACKNOWLEDGMENTS

I'd like to thank the women who were a crucial part in showing me what godly beauty is. Lynsey Rye, my spiritual big sis, I truly don't know where I'd be had I not met you in high school. What a life-changer and example you have been to me as I sat in your groups, discussed life with you over lunch dates at El Chapps, and joined you at the Becoming Conferences. I've also met so many amazing women through you in the community—too many to name but you know who you are!

To my teacher Mrs. Jaimes, who always took the time to "see me" and pour so much wisdom into my young mind. You taught me to celebrate how God had created me uniquely. You'll never know how much it meant. Thank you!

To Lexie Ward, Alyssa Stech, and Jessie Yonker. Many times over the years we sat around a campfire discussing our dreams, and each of you encouraged me to pursue my writing and speaking. Thank you for not only being the girls I laugh with the hardest but also the ones who keep me grounded. I'm beyond blessed to have you in my life. Cheers to Cadillac campfire conversations!

To Jess and Kristina for your lifelong friendship.

One minute we were playing house as little girls and now you are beautiful wives and moms that I look up to so much. There's just something about going through an entire lifetime as friends that creates a special bond, and I'm truly grateful for you!

To my Nana and Papa—you are the ones who make me feel the most special. You've dried my tears, cheered me on, and loved me unconditionally. You absolutely are my favorite people to spend time with because all feels right in the world when I'm with you. I can always count on you for a prayer, laugh, good meal, and, of course, a tube of lipstick.

To my amazing family: Mom, Dad, Andrea, Bill, Mike, Jalisa, Lauren, and Nate. I don't know how you put up with this wild-spirited, city-hopping, big-dreaming soul of mine, but you all do it so well. Thank you for loving and supporting me always. I've always felt the "You're crazy, but you're our crazy" love from you all. I thank God for you daily and still am not sure how I got so lucky to be placed in this family.

To all of my extended family for your constant belief and support.

To Uncle Tim and Aunt Cathy—the people who taught me about being a "mover and a shaker" in this world. I am beyond blessed to have spent time with you guys, having adventures in Michigan, working in your business, and gaining so much knowledge and encouragement throughout the years. You are a gift from God!

And finally to the amazing God-ordained group that has made this book possible! I'm blown away at the chance to work with such talented individuals.

To Tim Beals at Credo Communications. You saw the potential in this book long before it came to be or before the "platform" appeared. For that, I am forever grateful. Thank you for all of your expertise, care, and sharing in the excitement with me throughout the whole process!

A huge thank-you to my coauthor, Lorilee Craker. I knew I was lucky to have you as a coauthor when you signed off on your emails with the phrase "Big Hugs"! You have become a special friend and total inspiration to me. I will look back at our time working on this book while under the stars on an island as some of my most treasured memories! You are a rock star at what you do. Thank you—and Big Hugs!

To Keren Baltzer at FaithWords and her amazing team. How can I even begin to communicate my thanks?! Working with such an incredible publisher is proof to me there is a God who sees us. A God who orchestrates our crazy little human dreams into big, beautiful opportunities to use for His glory. Thank you for bringing this book into fruition and creating something that will bring glory to the kingdom.

NOTES

1. David Stoop. *Self-Talk: Key to Personal Growth.* (Grand Rapids: Revell, 1996).
2. Jennifer Garam, "Social Media Makes Me Feel Bad About Myself," *Psychology Today*, September 26, 2011, https://www.psychologytoday.com/blog/progress-not-perfection/201109/social-media-makes-me-feel-bad-about-myself.
3. Barb Roose, "Beautiful Devotional #5—Two Qualities That Make Every Woman Beautiful," BarbRoose.com, March 27, 2015, http://barbroose.com/beautiful-devotional-5-two-qualities-that-make-every-woman-beautiful/.
4. Danielle Pergament, "Exactly How Much Appearance Matters, According to Our National Judgment Survey," allure.com, February 10, 2016, http://www.allure.com/story/national-judgement-survey-statistics.
5. "Get the Facts on Eating Disorders," National Eating Disorders Association, accessed June 5, 2017, https://www.nationaleatingdisorders.org/get-facts-eating-disorders.
6. Hallie Graves, "Take it to a 2," comparedtowho.com, http://comparedtowho.me/2016/11/10/consumed-with-body-perfection/.

7. Christopher Hudspeth, "The Differences Between Cute, Pretty, Sexy & Beautiful," thoughtcatalog.com, January 22, 2014, http://thoughtcatalog.com/christopher-hudspeth/2014/01/the-differences-between-cute-pretty-sexy-beautiful/.

8. http://www.dictionary.com/browse/beautiful.

9. Mary DeMuth, "His Creation," *Christianity Today*, January 23, 2017, http://www.christianitytoday.com/women/devotions/2017/true-worth/his-creation.html.

10. "Only Two Percent of Women Describe Themselves as Beautiful: New Global Study Uncovers Desire for Broader Definition of Beauty," September 29, 2004, http://www.campaignforrealbeauty.com/press.asp?section=news&id=110.

11. Adam Grant, Ph D, "How to Think Like a Wise Person," *Psychology Today*, August 13, 2013, https://www.psychologytoday.com/blog/give-and-take/201308/how-think-wise-person.

12. Jeff Crosby, "James K.A. Smith—You Are What You Love [Feature Review]," *Englewood Review*, May 6, 2016, http://englewoodreview.org/james-k-a-smith-you-are-what-you-love-feature-review/.

13. Paula Spencer Scott, "Feeling Awe May Be the Secret to Health and Happiness," Parade.com, October 7, 2016, https://parade.com/513786/paulaspencer/feeling-awe-may-be-the-secret-to-health-and-happiness/.

14. Anthony de Mello. *The Song of the Bird*. (New York: Doubleday, 1982), 96.

15. Heather Creekmore, "Esther: Beauty for a Purpose," comparedtowho.com, http://comparedtowho.me/2017/01/09/esther-beauty-for-a-purpose/.

16. Jennie Allen. *Nothing to Prove*. (New York: Crown, 2017), 109.

17. Rick Warren. *The Purpose Driven Life.* (Grand Rapids: Zondervan, 2002).

18. Parker Palmer. *Let Your Life Speak: Listening for the Voice of Vocation.* (San Francisco: Jossey-Bass, 2000), 98-99.

ABOUT THE AUTHOR

ASHELY REITZ works with top agencies as a "curve model," offering her a platform to promote a healthy body image to young women. She has been an ambassador for a popular movement called Healthy Is the New Skinny and has been on the board for Miss SW Florida USA. Ashley has appeared in major magazines such as *Seventeen* and in national ad campaigns for Avon, Macy's, and Saks Fifth Avenue. Along with her "match" B.T., she was a fan favorite on FOX TV's reality show *Coupled*. Follow her at ashleyreitz.com.

LORILEE CRAKER is the author of thirteen books, including *Anne of Green Gables, My Daughter, and Me*; the CBA and ECPA bestseller *My Journey to Heaven* with Marvin J. Besteman; *Money Secrets of the Amish*; *A Is for Atticus: Baby Names from Great Books*, featured in *People* magazine; and the *New York Times* bestseller *Through the Storm* with Lynne Spears. In 2012 she was nominated for an Audie Award for best audio book in the personal development category. Follow her at lorileecraker.com.